AMERICAN PANTHER TANKS

AN EXAMINATION OF THE FIVE SURVIVING PANZER V TANKS INCLUDING THE RARE PANTHER II

CRAIG MOORE

FONTHILL

Fonthill Media Language Policy
Fonthill Media publishes in the international English language market. One language edition is published worldwide. As there are minor differences in spelling and presentation, especially with regard to American English and British English, a policy is necessary to define which form of English to use. The Fonthill Policy is to use the form of English native to the author. Craig Moore was born and educated in London, England; therefore, British English has been adopted in this publication.

Fonthill Media Limited
Fonthill Media LLC
www.fonthillmedia.com
office@fonthillmedia.com

First published in the United Kingdom and the United States of America 2021

British Library Cataloguing in Publication Data:
A catalogue record for this book is available from the British Library

ISBN 978-1-78155-804-1

Typeset in Minion Pro 10pt on 13pt
Printed and bound in England

CONTENTS

ACKNOWLEDGEMENTS

Herbert Ackermans, Tammam Khasawneh Abu Ahmad, Mark Barnes, Jason Belgrave, Pierre-Oliver Buan, Adrian Barrell, Lauren Child, Rob Cogan, Rob Collings, Ste Cork, Charles R. Lemons, Hilary Louis Doyle, Len Dyer, Daniel Enriquez, Massimo Foti, Marcus Hock, Jonathan Holt, Eugen Krings, Sue Moore, Brian Murdoch, Owen Myers, Steve Osfield, John Osselaer, Yuri Pasholok, John Pearson, Colin Rixon, Ramon Rijntjes, Lucian Stan, Steve Tatham, Ed Webster, Martin Webster, Ian Wilcox.

American Heritage Museum, Bovington Tank Museum, The Krings Collection, Kubinka Tank Museum, Musée des Blindés (Museum of Armour, Saumur, France), National Archives at Kew, US Army Armor and Cavalry Collection at Fort Benning, Overloon War Museum.

Three of the five surviving Panther tanks in America, awaiting their turn for restoration at Fort Benning, Georgia, USA. (© *U.S. Army Armor and Cavalry Collection*)

INTRODUCTION

American Panther Tanks sounds a strange title for a book, but currently, there are five surviving Second World War German Panther tanks in America. It is believed that fourteen captured Panzer V Panther tanks were shipped to the United States after the Second World War. Most were cut up and scrapped after being used for testing and targets on firing ranges.

The Panzer V Ausf. A Panther tank at the American Heritage Museum, Hudson, Massachusetts, near Boston, USA, has been completely restored to a very high standard. The other four Panther tanks are at Fort Benning, Columbus, Georgia, USA, under the care of the US Army Armor and Cavalry Collection (US AACC). They are awaiting their turn to be restored. They have over 300 vehicles in the Collection; around 100 have been cosmetically restored to stop further deterioration. At present (December 2020), they only have two members of staff. They are doing the best they can on a very limited budget.

If you are an American, please write to your local politician and ask that they lobby for a dramatic increase in the allotted budget so this very important historical collection can be preserved and eventually put on display to the public. At present, public access to this operational American Army base is only available on the few 'Open House' days. These are announced on the US Army Armor and Cavalry Collection Facebook page.

This book aims to provide a record of the condition of the tanks in April 2019 (when the photographs were taken) and explore the different and original external features on each tank that are still visible.

Panther tanks first saw action on the Eastern Front. They were also used in Italy, France, Belgium, and Holland. Panthers took part in the Ardennes offensive (the Battle of the Bulge) and the defence of Germany. It had better cross-country mobility than the Tiger tank and had similar hitting power, with its 7.5-cm KwK 42 L/70 long-barrelled, high-velocity anti-tank gun. Around 6,000 were produced.

The use of sloped armour kept the weight of the tank down but maintained its protection level. The angled front 80-mm armour glacis plate gave more protection than the Tiger tank's 100-mm vertical armour plate. This fact is not often mentioned. An enemy's standard armour-piercing round, fired from directly in front of the tank, hitting the glacis plate in a straight line, had to penetrate 139-mm (5.4 inches) of armour due to the angle of the armour. If the enemy tank was firing at the front of a Panther tank, but at a 45-degree angle to it, the shell would have to pass through 197 mm (7.7 inches) of armour.

Enemy tank crews always tried to outflank Panther tanks so as to fire at their more vulnerable side or rear armour. A German Panther tank crew's tactics involved presenting their frontal armour towards enemy tanks as much as possible.

Work on a replacement tank for the Panzer III and IV began in the early stages of the Second World War. In 1940, the design department of the German company MAN (*Maschinenfabrik* Augsburg-Nürnberg, meaning Machine Works of Augsburg and Nürnberg) was working on plans for the hull of a new 20-tonne class medium tank. The project was given a code VK.20.01 (M). The letter 'M' was an abbreviation for the company MAN. The letters 'VK' are an abbreviation '*Vollketten*' (fully tracked), followed by the weight class and the sub-variant. The later VK.30.01 identifies a fully tracked vehicle in the 30-tonne class variant 1, and the Panther prototype code VK.30.02 was the fully tracked variant 2 of the 30-tonne class design.

During Operation Barbarossa, the invasion of the Soviet Union, which started on Sunday, 22 June 1941, German forces encountered Soviet T–34 tanks for the first time. Battlefield reports were sent back to Berlin. They praised the Soviet tank's wide tracks, sloping armour, and powerful anti-tank gun. A panel of experts was sent to examine knocked-out T-34 tanks and speak with German tank crews. In early 1942, the German High Command issued new specifications for a 30-tonne class tank that included many of the same design features used on the T-34 tank. The Daimler-Benz design team worked on plans for the next German medium tank that met these specifications, in competition with the MAN company.

The Daimler-Benz design team tank used the design codename VK.30.02 (DB). They decided to use a traditional leaf-spring suspension system, large doubled roadwheels, no track return rollers, and a track drive sprocket at the rear. MAN used a similar suspension system as used on Henschel's Tiger design; its pairs of large, interleaved wheels provided their design with lower ground pressure as well as better traction and mobility.

The front glacis and lower hull armoured plates were sloped, as were the side panniers that covered the top of the wide tracks as well as the rear of the tank. The hull was narrower than the MAN design to keep the weight down, but this limited the size of the turret ring diameter and the size of the turret. It was 50 mm smaller than the MAN design. The internal space inside the hull and three-man turret was cramped. Daimler-Benz decided to use a new diesel engine where MAN used the same Maybach HL 210 P30 petrol/gasoline V12 water-cooled 650-hp engine that was currently in production and would be used in Henschel's Tiger tank hull design, thus reducing maintenance and logistics problems.

The Daimler-Benz design had their turret in a forward position very much like the Soviet T-34 tank. The MAN tank design had their turret more in the centre of the hull. As there was no space above the heads of the driver and radio operator in the Daimler-Benz tank design for escape hatches, two large circular hatches were inserted into the side armour, one on each side.

The Daimler-Benz designs used interlocking tenon wedge joints to make the junction between the front glacis and lower hull plate armour and the side pannier armour stronger. It was also used on the front of their turret. The MAN prototype design did not use this method. This would be a feature that would appear on the production Panther tank hull.

The design team at MAN incorporated sloping armour on the sides of the tank hull to cover wider tracks and steeper angled armour at the front of the vehicle hull as per the German Army design requirements. These features can be seen on drawings dated 2 May 1942, with the codename VK.30.02 (M). These plans also incorporated the proposed turret designed by the German company Rheinmetall-Borsig, which was armed with a 7.5-cm KwK 42 L/70 anti-tank gun.

The German words for experimental trial series are *Versuchs-Serie*. This is why the two MAN Panther tank hull prototypes were given the designation V1 and V2. At first, a large metal weighted box was fitted on top of the V1 hull instead of the turret while it underwent cross-country trials. Later, the Rheinmetall-Borsig turret was fitted to both V1 and V2 tanks. Both were ready for tests by September 1942.

German High Command wanted the new Panther tank in production by December 1942 so that there would be enough numbers available for the spring and summer offensives of 1943. In May 1942, the Daimler-Benz VK.30.02 (DB) and the MAN VK.30.02 (M) paper designs were submitted.

The MAN design eventually won the contract because of several issues with the Daimler-Benz design. The major ones were that its turret was not ready for production. Its hull was too small to mount the approved larger Rheinmetall-Borsig turret. It did not use an engine that was already being produced and fitted in other tanks. This would have caused a logistics problem as well as manufacturing delays. The suspension system and wider tracks of the MAN design gave a lower ground pressure reading.

It should be noted that the MAN tank hull prototype design did not use the robust interlocking tenon joint design on its armour plate junctions. This Daimler-Benz feature was added to the final production design. Both the V1 and V2 prototypes displayed numerous minor design aspects that were not used in the production Panther. The two prototype vehicles were used to test different features before starting a production run.

The first production Panzer V Panther tank was the Ausf. D, not the Ausf. A. This confuses many people. In the past, German tank versions started with the letter 'A' and then went on to 'B', 'C', 'D', etc. In January 1943, MAN produced the first production series Panther Ausf. D tank. 'Ausf.' is an abbreviation for the German word '*Ausführung*', which means version. The Panzer V Ausf. D Panther tank *Fahrgestell-Nummer Serie* hull numbers range from 210001 to 210254 and 211001 to 213220.

Daimler-Benz had been the favourite to gain the contract for production of the Panther, and administratively, the Ausf. D designation was used in official reports. Later, the *Waffenamt* changed its opinion in favour of the MAN design, which was put into production. As the designation *Ausführung*. D was already in use, it was decided to keep it like that.

1

PANTHER II TANK AT FORT BENNING

The Panther II hull fitted with a Panzer V Ausf. G turret armed with a 7.5-cm KwK 42/1 L/70 anti-tank gun under cover in a Fort Benning tank shelter. (© *U.S. Army Armor and Cavalry Collection*)

The Panther II tank was being designed before the first Panther Ausf. D saw combat on the Eastern Front in mid-1943. Hitler had expressed concerns about the thickness of the Panther tank's armour, so work was started on developing a new Panther tank with thicker armour and a hull design that could be manufactured faster and cheaper.

THE SOVIET ANTI-TANK RIFLE MENACE

The threat from Soviet infantry anti-tank rifles had to be solved. During the Second World War, on the Eastern Front, the Soviet Army was issued with PTRD-41 anti-tank rifles and the similar but semi-automatic 'Simonov' PTRS-41 anti-tank rifle. They fired armour-piercing BS-41 14.5-mm rounds that had a muzzle velocity of 1,020 m/s and could penetrate 30–35 mm of armour at a distance of 300 m and 40-mm-thick armour at 100 m. It was an armour-piercing incendiary round with a carbide-tungsten core. The Panther Ausf. D tank only had 40-mm-thick hull side armour and 30-mm rear hull armour. Soviet anti-tank rifles knocked out very few German tanks, but many were damaged internally by rounds penetrating the armour. Crewmen were killed or suffered injuries from flying metal inside the tank's fighting compartment. Sometimes, a lucky shot would cause a fire or ignite stored ammunition.

During the invasion of Poland in September 1939, Soviet tanks had been knocked out by Polish Model 35 anti-tank rifles. They captured hundreds of these weapons. Soviet weapons designer Vasily Degtyaryov incorporated the design of its lock and a number of features from the German *Panzerbüchse* 38 (PzB 38), a man-portable single-shot, manually loaded anti-tank rifle with a recoiling barrel, to produce a new Soviet weapon. The PTRD-41 anti-tank rifle was simpler to manufacture than the more complicated PTRS-41; this allowed for faster mass production of the PTRD-41.

On 26 October 1941, the first 300 PTRD-41 anti-tank rifles left the Degtyaryov Plant in Kovrov, 120 miles east of Moscow, and were sent to the 16th Army, who were on the front line guarding Moscow. It only required one man to carry the rifle. The rifle could be disassembled into two parts to reduce its length, making it easier to carry or store on a train or truck. The ammunition was put in a shoulder bag. Loading and firing the weapon was simple. The rumours that the recoil was so bad that it would break a man's collarbone were false. At the end of the barrel, a small muzzle brake was fitted to dissipate the energy of the explosive gasses which helped reduce recoil. The end of the stock on the PTRD was padded. The iron gun sights were offset on the left of the rifle with two settings: 0–400 meters and 400–1,000 meters. Left-handed soldiers could not easily fire this weapon.

The PTRD-41 had a rate of fire of eight–ten rounds a minute, but the semi-automatic PTDS had a rate of fire of fifteen rounds a minute. It was found that the weapon was also useful when deployed against fortified machine-gun nests. A 14.5-mm round was capable of punching a hole through concrete up to 20 cm thick at a range of 800 m. It was effective against soft-skinned and thinly armoured vehicles at ranges of up to 1,000 m.

In early 1942, front-line Soviet troops had access to 8,116 PTRS-41 and PTRD-41 anti-tank rifles. By July 1942, this figure had risen to 65,365, and by 1 January 1943, 118,563 had been issued. Although these weapons by this time could no longer penetrate the frontal armour of German tanks, the sheer number available made them a viable threat as the 14.5-mm round was capable of penetrating most of the German panzer's hull sides including the Panther tank.

THE PANTHER II TANK'S ARMOUR

The thickness of the Panther II tank's side hull armour was planned to be increased from 40 mm, as found on the Panther Ausf. D, to 60 mm. The front glacis plate was strengthened by the use of 100-mm-thick armour rather than the 80-mm armour used on the Panther Ausf. D. The turret armour was also to be increased at the front from 80 to 100 mm (this was later increased) and sides from 45 to 60 mm. This was listed in a report dated 22 January 1943. Armour this thick would keep the crew safe from direct hits by Soviet 14.5-mm anti-tank rifle rounds.

DEVELOPMENT

Two were ordered, but only one prototype hull was completed. That Panther II hull is now part of the American Armor and Cavalry Collection at Fort Benning, Georgia. It is fitted with a Panther Ausf. G turret.

Initially, the production plan contained in a report dated 22 January 1943 was to start Panther II production in September 1943. This never happened. Notes for a meeting that took place on 10 February 1943 recorded the decision to put the Panther II straight into production without building an experimental series of vehicles first. This was not standard practice.

On 17 February 1943, during a meeting at the *Reichsministerium*, the German Army *Heereswaffenamt* WaPrüf 6/111 looked at the problem as a lack of commonality in tank parts. It would ease the logistics supply problem if different tanks used the same components. They instructed Henschel and MAN to cooperate on the design of the Tiger *Ausführung* B (Tiger II) and the proposed Panther II tank hulls.

On 27 February 1944, a *Führer* directive ordered that the designation *Panzerkampfwagen* V tank would be dropped, and the tank would be known as the 'Panther'.

On 29 March 1943, a decision was made at a meeting of the *Hauptausschuss* that postponed the start of Panther II production in September 1943 to an unspecified date at the end of 1944 or the beginning of 1945. The Panther I was to continue in production throughout 1943 and 1944. This decision did not officially cancel the Panther II project; it just postponed its commencement. The Panther II never entered production.

On 5 April 1943, it was recorded at a meeting in the *Panzerkommission* that the MAN factory informed them that the first Panther II Prototype hull would be completed by mid-August 1943. This prototype was completed and is now housed at the US Army Armor and Cavalry Collection at Fort Benning, Georgia.

On 20 April 1943, at a meeting in the *Reichsministerium*, the findings of development work on how to give greater protection to the Panther I side armour were submitted. They found that the use of *Schürzen* sufficiently decreased the risk of penetration of the hull armour by Soviet 14.5-mm anti-tank rifles. The requirement for an increase in the hull side armour (with the detrimental increase in weight and strain on the tank engine and suspension) was no longer a matter of priority. The main driving force for the need to develop the Panther II with its thicker heavier armour no longer existed.

A recommendation after a meeting at the MAN factory on 4 May 1943 was that the Panther II tank should not enter mass production at this time, but improvements gained from the Panther II project were to be incorporated in future Panther I tank designs. In June 1943, companies that had been told to prepare to start producing the Panther II were now informed that they would be building the Panther I for the foreseeable future.

SUSPENSION

The running gear used on the Panther II design made use of the Tiger *Ausführung* B (Tiger II) tank parts. This part's commonality would help with the supply of spare parts and make production more streamlined. Due to the limited supply of rubber, it was intended to fit them with the same *gummisparenden Laufwerk* (steel-tyre, rubber-cushioned, rubber-saving road-wheels), which were 800 mm in diameter. The idler wheel and track arrangement of the Panther II were also very similar to the Tiger II, but the Panther II would only have seven road-wheels, whereas the longer Tiger II would have nine road-wheels. It used the same single torsion bar suspension system.

TANK TRACKS

The Panther II hull is fitted with tank tracks that have two guide teeth. The road-facing track link has chevrons included in the design for extra grip. These same tracks were used as transportation tracks for the King Tiger tank. Their designation is GG 24/660/300 (Test track, type 24, width 660-mm, spacing 300-mm). The track pin fitted on the Panther II hull is the same length as the track link. The end does not protrude out of the link. Unlike most German track pins, these pins are not retained in place by a split pin. If a track pin came loose, it would be hit back in place each time it passed the track pin bump on the side of the tank hull. This configuration is very similar to the system used on many Soviet Second World War tanks.

It was found that the two guide teeth were too weak when used with the *gummisparenden Laufwerk*. The Panther track already in use with the Panzer V Ausf. D Panther standard rubber-rimmed wheels also suffered from broken guide teeth. It was proposed that a different type of track was forged for use on the production version of the Panther II. It was to consist of a cast track link with one stronger guide tooth and two cleats with a forged *Zwischenglied* (connection link). These were not made as the Panther II did not enter production.

DRIVER AND RADIO OPERATOR

The Panther II had a steering wheel in place of steering levers. Both the driver and radio operator had a rotating periscope above their heads. It had an armoured rain cover. There were no vision slits in the front glacis plate, just an armoured ball-mounted machine gun mount. The entry hatches on the hull deck look similar to those used on the Panther Ausf. D or Ausf. A but not those fitted on the Ausf. G.

POWER UNIT

The Panther II was powered by a Maybach HL 230 P30 V-12, water-cooled 23-litre petrol/gasoline 600-hp (at 2,500 rpm) engine. On 5 March 1943, to help with vehicle maintenance, it was decided that the final drive and steering units would be designed to be removed and installed independent of each other. The Maybach OLVAR or ZF AK 7-200 all-synchro-mesh gearbox was chosen to be fitted on both the Panther II and King Tiger. The Tiger's L 801-controlled regenerative steering mechanism was also chosen to be installed in the Panther II.

TANK BELLY

The Panther II belly armour is in three sections. The front part is made from 30-mm-thick armour plate. The middle and rear sections are only 16 mm thick to help keep the total weight down. The rear-towing bracket is bolted to the rear armoured plate but also to the rear belly plate.

TURRET

Several turret designs were submitted for the Panther II tank hull but not completed. Rheinmetall designed a new turret for the Panther Ausf. G tank. The plans were dated 7 November 1943 and labelled H-SKA 86176 '*Turm Panther 2 schmale Blendenausführung*' (narrow mantlet variant Panther 2 turret). An amended version dated 1 March 1944 and labelled H-Sk 88517 '*Turm-Panther schmale Blende*' (narrow mantlet Panther turret) was also submitted. WaPrüf 6 was not happy with the designs.

At the beginning of 1944, the design contract was passed over to Daimler-Benz. Their smaller *Schmalturm* (narrow turret) was designed for the proposed Panther Ausf. F and also intended to be fitted on the Panther II. The surface area at the front of the turret was minimised, but the armour protection was increased without adding too much weight. The turret weighed less than the original Panther turret—7,565 kg compared to 7,665 kg.

The gun mantlet was no longer curved. It was replaced by a single slab of 120-mm armour placed at a slight 12-degree angle. This eliminated the Panther tank 'shot trap', where enemy armour-piercing rounds were deflected downwards off the curved gun mantlet into the hull roof, killing the driver or radio operator. Production time was estimated to be reduced by 30–40 per cent. It was made from rolled steel plate, and unlike the curved gun mantlet, it did not require a specialised manufacturing process.

The coaxial 7.92-mm MG 34 machine gun was going to be replaced with a 7.92-mm MG 42, which had a muzzle velocity of 740 m/s and could fire 1,500 rounds per minute. It would have been fired out of a hole in the front turret armoured plate on the left side of the gun. This opening had a semi-circular rain guard. The machine gun mount was attached to the main gun cradle. There were two ammunition containers attached below the gun. One contained live ammunition while the other was used to collect spent cartridges.

It was fitted with a horizontal stereoscopic rangefinder; each lens was placed in its protective armoured bulge on the side of the turret. The gunner had an armoured protected periscope gunsight above his position in the turret roof to the left of the gun.

The recoil mechanism on the 7.5-cm *Kampfwagenkanone* (KwK) tank gun was moved to beneath the gun barrel. It was given the designation 7.5-cm KwK 44/1 L70. It was developed by Škoda Pilsen. The initial guns fitted to the turrets had muzzle brakes, but there were no plans to fit muzzle brakes to the gun barrels if the turret went into production. The gun would have had -8 degrees of depression and +20 degrees of elevation.

The commander's domed cupola was lower in height compared to previous Panther turret domed cupolas with the object of reducing the tank's profile. It had seven periscope housings to give the commander all-round vision. They could easily be replaced under combat conditions from inside the turret. The periscopes were bullet-resistant, not bulletproof, and were often damaged and needed swapping. Spare periscopes would have been kept in the turret. A ring was fixed externally on the cupola. It could mount infrared night fighting lights, an anti-aircraft AA gun, or a scissor-type scope.

A large circular crew hatch was installed at the rear of the turret. It had a semi-circular rain guard mounted over the hatch. A long handle was welded above the hatch to help the crew get in and out of the hatch. A pistol port was added to the top right side of the hatch. The crew could check that it was safe to get out of the back of the turret before they opened the hatch. If there were enemy infantry waiting for them on the engine deck, they could fire their personal firearms at them.

Daimler-Benz, in cooperation with Škoda, developed the new smaller *Schmalturm* narrow turret design and built several experimental turrets to test different features. Only one survived. It was rescued from a firing range and is now on display at the Tank Museum, Bovington, Dorset, England.

Daimler-Benz was in the process of looking how to mount an 8.8-cm KwK 43 L/71 gun with a stabilised gunsight in the same turret. Only a wooden mock-up was constructed.

PRODUCTION

The Panther II never entered production. As already mentioned, the main reasons for the start of the Panther II development program was the fear that the current Panther, the Ausf. D, would be vulnerable to Soviet infantry 14.5-mm anti-tank rifles. However, the implementation of *Schürzen* removed the threat from anti-tank rifles and reduced the need for a thicker-armoured, heavier Panther tank variant.

The desire to change the original Panther II design to include additional features extended the expected completion date to August 1944. Some of the new elements that were under consideration for inclusion in the final tank were a track system that had one single stronger guide tooth, a new track tensioning system, the mounting of the Tiger II final drive, and an improved steering gear that would have required a redesign of the lower hull plate from 55 to 50 degrees.

Some design lessons learnt from the Panther II development were later incorporated in the Panther Ausf. G hull. No document has yet been found that states the Panther II project was officially cancelled. Plans for the start of production of the Panther II were postponed.

THE SURVIVING PANTHER II HULL

This Panther II was formerly displayed at Aberdeen Proving Grounds (APG) and then the Patton Cavalry and Armor Museum at Fort Knox. It is made from soft steel and is a prototype.

The tank was shipped from Europe without a turret. In its place was fitted a large test weight ring to simulate the weight of a turret. A Panther Ausf. G turret (Fgst.Nr. 121447) was installed onto the Panther II hull at APG. It had an original drive sprocket on the left side and an improved drive sprocket on the right side. It was missing the hull deck and hatches over the driver and radio operator's position. A spare section of decking with hatches from a Panther Ausf. G was fitted over the hole. Most likely, the vehicle came from the Smithsonian Institute, which had requested vehicles from the US Army.

In the mid-1960s, APG transferred ownership of several tanks to the Smithsonian Institute, as they were planning to build another museum like the National Aviation Museum but for combat vehicles. The project never took off, and the vehicles stayed at APG. The Smithsonian Institute offered them to the Patton Museum. The vehicles were transported from APG to Fort Knox.

The Panther II came to the Patton Museum of Cavalry and Armor in the early 1970s. The original engine was replaced by one in running order at the Boatwright tank overhaul facility at Fort Knox; it came from the 'Munich' Panther Ausf. G (Fgst.Nr. 121455) already located at Fort Knox. One final drive was also repaired. The 'Munich' Panther Ausf. G. is also part of the US Army Armor and Cavalry Collection.

When the Panther II hull first arrived in Aberdeen, it still had one 'improved' sprocket wheel on the right side of the tank and one 'original' sprocket wheel on the left side. The 'original' sprocket with the wider teeth was replaced with an 'improved' sprocket with slimmer, less angled teeth when the tank was restored to running condition at the Patton Museum. After repairs were completed, the tank was in a drivable condition and used for demonstrations for several years.

When the Patton Museum closed, it was transferred to the US Army Armor and Cavalry Collection at Fort Benning, Georgia.

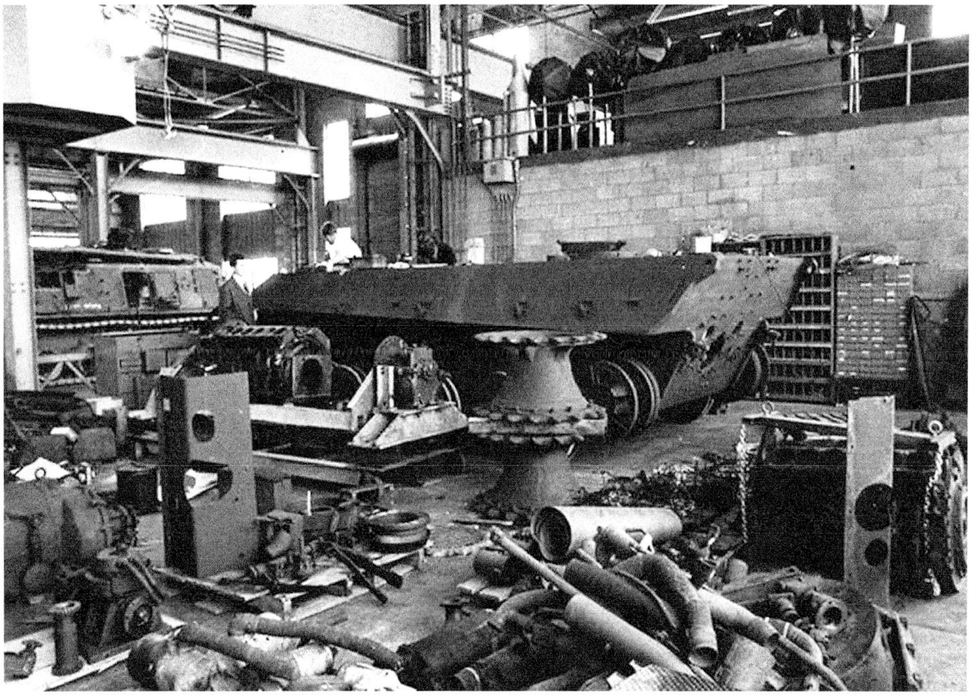

The Panther II hull in the Boatwright tank overhaul facility at Fort Knox, Kentucky, USA. (© *U.S. Army Armor and Cavalry Collection*)

The Panther II hull fitted with a Panzer V Ausf. G turret at Aberdeen Proving Grounds, Maryland, USA. Notice that the left-side front sprocket wheel has the wider triangular track teeth. (© *U.S. Army Armor and Cavalry Collection*)

PANTHER II SPECIFICATIONS	
Dimensions (L-W-H)	8.95 m × 3.28 m × 2.94 m (29 feet 4 inches × 10 feet 9 inches × 9 feet 8 inches)
Total weight	50 tonnes
Main Armament	7.5-cm KwK 44/1 L/70, 82 rounds
Secondary Armament	2 × 7.92-mm MG 34 machine guns
Armour: front upper glacis	100 mm at 55 degrees
Armour: front lower hull	60 mm at 50 degrees
Armour: hull side	60 mm at 0 degrees
Armour: side superstructure	60 mm at 30 degrees
Armour: rear	40 mm at 30 degrees
Armour: pannier bottom armour	16 mm at 90 degrees
Armour: engine deck armour	25 mm at 90 degrees
Armour: hull deck armour	40-25 mm at 90 degrees
Armour: belly hull armour	16–30 mm at 90 degrees
Schmalturm turret front armour	120 mm at 12 degrees
Schmalturm turret side armour	60 mm at 25 degrees
Schmalturm turret rear armour	60 mm at 25 degrees
Schmalturm turret roof armour	40 mm at 90 degrees
Schmalturm turret mantlet armour	150 mm curved
Crew	5 (commander, driver, gunner, loader, radioman/machine gunner)
Propulsion	Maybach HL 230 P30 V12 water-cooled 600-hp petrol/gasoline engine
Transmission	ZF AK 7-200 7-forward/1-reverse gearbox
Suspensions	Single torsion bars
Max Road Speed	46 km/h (28.5 mph)
Operational range	200 km (124 miles)
Production	One prototype hull

The Panther II Hull was designed before the Panzer V Ausf. G. The design of the later production tank Ausf. G hull incorporated many of the features of the Panther II hull. The large fuel tank at the back stayed the same shape. Notice on the Panther II and Ausf. G the side armour got wider at the back. One straight edge was quicker to produce. (© *U.S. Army Armor and Cavalry Collection*)

The rear of the Panther II hull is missing stowage bins, the 20-tonne jack, and some smaller fixtures. It is fitted with the welded rectangular armoured exhaust covers that were used on the later Ausf. G Panther, rather than the curved cast exhaust covers. (© *U.S. Army Armor and Cavalry Collection*)

Left rear three-quarter view of the Panther II. The holes at the back of the side armour at the top are used to lift the hull up by a crane or winch. (© *U.S. Army Armor and Cavalry Collection*)

Right rear three-quarter view of the Panther II. The tools and stowage boxes are not fitted to the back of the tank. The exhaust pipes are recent additions. They seem too tall. On the original photos of the Panther II after its capture, the exhaust pipes were shorter. (© *U.S. Army Armor and Cavalry Collection*)

Front three-quarter view of the Panther II. There are holes in the side armour at the front of the tank by the glacis plate. They were used to lift the hull up by a crane or winch. They are also used to help tow the vehicle or tow another vehicle that had suffered a mechanical failure. (© *U.S. Army Armor and Cavalry Collection*)

The glacis plate armour was 100 mm thick on the hull of the Panther II. (© *U.S. Army Armor and Cavalry Collection*)

The glacis plate armour was 80 mm thick on the hulls of the Panzer V Ausf. D, Ausf. A, and Ausf. G tanks. (© *U.S. Army Armor and Cavalry Collection*)

The side armour was 60 mm thick on the hull of the Panther II. (© *U.S. Army Armor and Cavalry Collection*)

The side armour was 40 mm thick on the hulls of the Panzer V Ausf. D, Ausf. A, and Ausf. G tanks. (© *U.S. Army Armor and Cavalry Collection*)

The hulls of the Panther Ausf. D and early production Panther Ausf. A had the 'letterbox' machine gun opening in the glacis plate. The Panther II hull had a ball mount for the 7.92-mm MG 34 machine gun. The ball mount was protected by a spherical armoured guard. To prevent bullet splinters flying up the glacis plate and jamming the ball mount, two ridges were built into the bottom of the guard. (© *U.S. Army Armor and Cavalry Collection*)

Scheinwerfer mit Tarnkappe (headlight with camouflage cover). On the Panzer V Ausf. D Panther tank, a headlight was mounted on the glacis plate. It was much easier and quicker to produce the Panther tank if the headlights were fixed to the forward track guard like on the Panther II. This feature was included on the future Panzer V Ausf. G Panther tank design. (© *U.S. Army Armor and Cavalry Collection*)

The rear view of the *Scheinwerfer mit Tarnkappe* (headlight with camouflage cover) on the Panther II tank front left track guard. The right-side track guard did not have a headlight. (© *U.S. Army Armor and Cavalry Collection*)

The front track guards were held in position at the top hinge and by a bolted bracket into the top of the side hull armour where it meets the glacis plate. The hole in the side hull armour was used for towing. It was also used when the tank had to be lifted by a crane or winch. (© *U.S. Army Armor and Cavalry Collection*)

This photograph was taken at the front of the Panther II tank. Two rectangular cuts in the hull armour have been used to strengthen the weld joint with the armoured casting for the final drive housing. (© *U.S. Army Armor and Cavalry Collection*)

Top left-side rectangular interlocking armour weld joint between the 100-mm-thick glacis plate and the 60-mm hull side armour plate. (© *U.S. Army Armor and Cavalry Collection*)

Lower left-side rectangular interlocking armour weld joint between the 100-mm-thick glacis plate and the 60-mm hull side armour plate. (© *U.S. Army Armor an-d Cavalry Collection*)

Right-side rectangular interlocking armour weld joints between the 100-mm-thick glacis plate and the 60-mm lower hull armour plate. (© *U.S. Army Armor and Cavalry Collection*)

The central rectangular interlocking armour weld joint between the 100-mm-thick glacis plate and the 60-mm lower hull armour plate. (© *U.S. Army Armor and Cavalry Collection*)

Left-side rectangular interlocking armour weld joint between the 100-mm-thick glacis plate and the 60-mm lower hull armour plate. (© *U.S. Army Armor and Cavalry Collection*)

The first and last *Schürzen* plates on both sides were held in place by clips. The brackets can be seen on the side of the upper hull superstructure. None of the standard equipment-holding brackets were fitted to the superstructure sides on this prototype. (© *U.S. Army Armor and Cavalry Collection*)

The *Schürzen* brackets went all along the length of the side of the superstructure armour. (© *U.S. Army Armor and Cavalry Collection*)

The *Schürzen* bracket over the front-drive sprocket wheel. (© *U.S. Army Armor and Cavalry Collection*)

The weld joint between the rear armour plate and the side superstructure armour plate was strengthened by the inclusion of a mortice and tenon joints at the rear. The final *Schürzen* bracket at the back of the tank was different to the others. It was a simple L-shaped bracket. The circular hole at the top of the side armour plate was used to lift the tank hull by a crane or winch. (© *U.S. Army Armor and Cavalry Collection*)

The armour underneath the pannier was 16 mm thick—the same thickness as used on the standard production Panther tanks. The vertical hull side armour was 60 mm thick. This was 20 mm thicker than that used on the standard production Panther tanks. (© *U.S. Army Armor and Cavalry Collection*)

The track pin return plate—a bump in the side of the wall—would knock the track pins back into place if they got loose. On early production Panther Ausf. A tanks, this style of plate was located beneath the shock absorber mounting pinhead—the round item in the photograph. It was replaced by the much simpler rectangular designed plate, mounted in front of the idler, on later production models. (© *U.S. Army Armor and Cavalry Collection*)

The front-drive sprocket now fitted to the front left side of the Panther II is the later style of drive sprocket with the square-shaped gap between the teeth. It is from a different tank. The earlier version had a V-shaped gap and was fitted to the left side of the tank when it arrived in America. This was replaced. (© *U.S. Army Armor and Cavalry Collection*)

The front-drive sprocket fitted to the front right side of the Panther II also had the later style of wheel with the square-shaped gap between the teeth. This was the type of sprocket wheel that was fitted to the right side of the tank when it arrived in America. (© *U.S. Army Armor and Cavalry Collection*)

The five bolts connect the final drive housing on the front left side of the tank to the side hull armour. Notice that rectangular mortice interlocking joints. These made the welded joint stronger. The flat circular heads of the track pins can be seen linking the track link with its two chevroned, road-facing treads and the connection link. (© *U.S. Army Armor and Cavalry Collection*)

This is the inside view of the right-side final drive housing and hull weld joint. The belly plate at the front of the tank can be seen under the tank. The front section was 30 mm thick, followed by two 16-mm plates. The final drive of the Panther II is that of the Tiger II, and this also meant the lower hull armoured plate was at 50-degree angle, not 55 degrees as on the Panther Ausf. D. Following the postponement of Panther II production, conversion to the Tiger II final drive was still being pursued. Studies were made on how to incorporate it into the Panther hull. (© *U.S. Army Armor and Cavalry Collection*)

The tank track links fitted on the Panther II hull had two guide teeth that fitted into the groove in the *gummisparenden Laufwerk* road-wheels. (© *U.S. Army Armor and Cavalry Collection*)

Here you can see the groove in one of the steel tyre road-wheels where the track's guide tooth slotted into. (© *U.S. Army Armor and Cavalry Collection*)

This shows how the road facing track links, with the two inward-facing guide teeth, were locked together with the *Zwischenglied* (connection link) by the track pin. The tracks that would be used on the production Panther II would have been the *Verladekette* (transportation tracks) used on the Tiger II, type Gg 24/660/300. (© *U.S. Army Armor and Cavalry Collection*)

The *gummisparendenden Laufwerk* road-wheels were interleaved. The rear road-wheels slotted into the back guide tooth on the tank's track and the front road-wheels slotted into the forward guide tooth. Notice there are no return rollers. The spacing of the Panther II road-wheels was a bit odd. As it only had seven road-wheels, the rear last axle on the right side and the last and second to last on the left side were placed further back, creating a gap on both sides. The Panther Ausf. D had eight road-wheels evenly spaced, as did all other production Panthers. The original 860-mm Panther road-wheels were larger in diameter than these 800-mm rubber-saving steel tyre road-wheels. Why it was opted to go with seven road-wheels for the Panther II is not clear. (© *U.S. Army Armor and Cavalry Collection*)

The track pins used on the Panther II were not kept in place by a split pin. They were the same length as the track and did not protrude out. The idler wheel was at the rear of the Panther II hull. The Panther II idler wheel at first glance looks identical or very similar to that of the Tiger II Ausf. B, but the latter had six spokes where the Panther II has eight. The hub on the Panther II has six bolts, whereas on the Tiger II Ausf. B, there were eight. (*© U.S. Army Armor and Cavalry Collection*)

The turret is from a late production Panther Ausf. G tank (Fgst.Nr. 121455). It was transferred to the Panther II hull in Fort Knox, America. It was fitted with a 'chin' mantlet that was designed to reduce the chances of an armour-piercing round ricocheting downwards into the crew compartment. The interlocking straight edge mortice armour welds made the joint stronger. (*© U.S. Army Armor and Cavalry Collection*)

On 24 January 1945, the MAN factory was ordered to stop welding the anti-aircraft gun mount circular ring on top of the commander's cupola. Starting in March 1945, a metal post was welded on top of the front left side facing cupola periscope armoured guard on late production Panther Ausf. G turrets. This was to serve as a base for a new swivelling anti-aircraft gun mount. (*© U.S. Army Armor and Cavalry Collection*)

When the commander unlocked the hatch from inside the turret, it would spring upwards and could then be swung across the cupola and be locked in place on the side. This style of hatch reduced the profile of the tank. Many British and Soviet tank hatches flipped upwards; this movement could be seen by the enemy. The slot in the armour is a rain gully to drain water away from the hatch seal. (© *U.S. Army Armor and Cavalry Collection*)

This is the external catch for the lock on the commander's cupola hatch. (© *U.S. Army Armor and Cavalry Collection*)

On the forward-facing section of the cupola, a gun sighting vane was welded to the cupola's curved side on a T-shaped bracket. The sighting vane is a gun laying tool that consisted of two triangles. The rear one had a 'V' cut into the top and was used to line up with the tip of the forward vane like on a normal iron gun sight. This helped the commander to see where the tank's gun was pointing and whether it was facing the right target. (© *U.S. Army Armor and Cavalry Collection*)

The horseshoe-shaped raised armoured guard in front of the cupola protects the opening where the infrared night vision unit's steel band, which indicated elevation, entered the turret. (© *U.S. Army Armor and Cavalry Collection*)

This clamp on the front right side of the turret is for holding a *Losterkennungstafeln* (poison-gas detection card). Two others were welded on to the turret in locations that were visible from the commander's cupola when the hatch was locked in the closed position. (© *U.S. Army Armor and Cavalry Collection*)

The second clamp on the front left side of the turret is also for holding a *Losterkennungstafeln*. (© *U.S. Army Armor and Cavalry Collection*)

The third clamp is on the rear right side of the turret. It is for holding a *Losterkennungstafeln*. (© *U.S. Army Armor and Cavalry Collection*)

This armoured cast dome on the turret roof protects the exhaust fan. The semi-circular guard in front protects the side openings and stops bullets and shrapnel entering the side openings. (© *U.S. Army Armor and Cavalry Collection*)

This is the rear view of the armoured cast dome on the turret roof that protects the exhaust fan. (© *U.S. Army Armor and Cavalry Collection*)

The 360-degree *Nahverteidigungswaffe* (close protection weapon) grenade and smoke round launcher was attached to the turret roof at the rear right side. It was loaded and operated from inside the turret. (© *U.S. Army Armor and Cavalry Collection*)

Three U-shaped lifting eyes were welded to the top of the turret, two at the front and one at the rear. Chains were attached to them when the turret needed to be lifted off the tank hull. The small triangular brace added to the rear lifting lug is the only difference, at start of production, between an Ausf. A and an Ausf. G turret. (© *U.S. Army Armor and Cavalry Collection*)

A long sheet of metal was welded over the gap between the front turret armour and the gun mantlet to stop rain and debris entering and jamming the movement of the gun. (© *U.S. Army Armor and Cavalry Collection*)

The left side of the gun mantlet had a post and a circular cap, which looked very similar to the end of a big nail. There was one on the other side. These were used for lifting the gun mantlet off the turret for repairs. The thin rain and debris guard can be seen on the top. (*© U.S. Army Armor and Cavalry Collection*)

The right side of the gun mantlet also has a lifting post at the top. Below it are two brackets welded on to the armour. A rectangular length of metal, on which were the plug sockets for the infrared optics system, was bolted onto these brackets. (*© U.S. Army Armor and Cavalry Collection*)

Starting in September 1944, the gunsight aperture rain guard was lengthened as rainwater was still entering the hole. This monocular gunsight on the left of the gun has the lengthened version. (*© U.S. Army Armor and Cavalry Collection*)

This is the coaxial 7.92-mm MG 34 machine gun aperture on the right side of the gun mantlet. (© *U.S. Army Armor and Cavalry Collection*)

This block of metal welded to the top of the turret at the front is the gun mantlet top bump stop. The rain and debris guard is cut around it. (© *U.S. Army Armor and Cavalry Collection*)

The V-shaped block of metal welded to the front of the turret on the left side at the bottom is the gun mantlet bottom bump stop. (© *U.S. Army Armor and Cavalry Collection*)

The V-shaped block of metal welded to the front of the turret on the right side at the bottom is the gun mantlet bottom bump stop. (© *U.S. Army Armor and Cavalry Collection*)

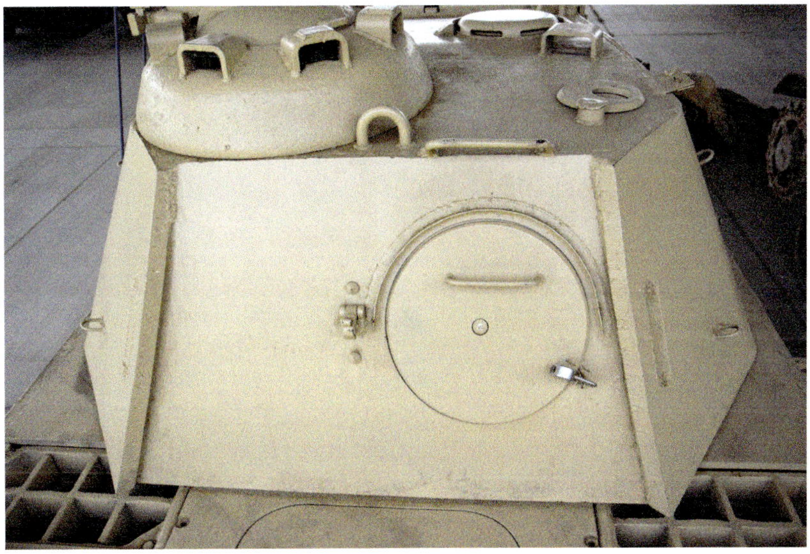

Starting in June 1944, a handle was welded onto the back of the large circular escape hatch at the rear of the turret. (© *U.S. Army Armor and Cavalry Collection*)

The top of the rear turret hatch seal was protected by a rain guard. The silver-coloured lock is modern. (© *U.S. Army Armor and Cavalry Collection*)

Left column:
The rear turret hatch lock was welded onto the armour plate between the two cone-shaped bolts that secured the hatch hinge on the inside of the turret. (© *U.S. Army Armor and Cavalry Collection*)

When the commander's cupola hatch was open, he could use this gun laying sight. It was a metal post welded onto the back of the forward-facing periscope armoured cover. (© *U.S. Army Armor and Cavalry Collection*)

The loops used to run wire or rope to secure camouflage material can be seen on the side of the turret. These started to be fitted on Panther tank turrets built at the end of December 1944 onwards. Five were fitted to each side of the turret. The exception was on turrets built by Daimler-Benz. They never added these loops to their Panther Ausf. G turrets. (© *U.S. Army Armor and Cavalry Collection*)

Right column:
A muzzle brake was fitted to the 7.5-cm KwK 42 L/70 tank gun. They were designed to increase the length of time the barrel could be used before it needed changing. The muzzle brake deflected a proportion of the explosive gasses sideways which reduced the pressure inside the barrel and reduced gun recoil. The weight of the muzzle brake also reduces muzzle rise. (© *U.S. Army Armor and Cavalry Collection*)

On this top view of the Panther's muzzle brake, you can see the securing bolt. (© *U.S. Army Armor and Cavalry Collection*)

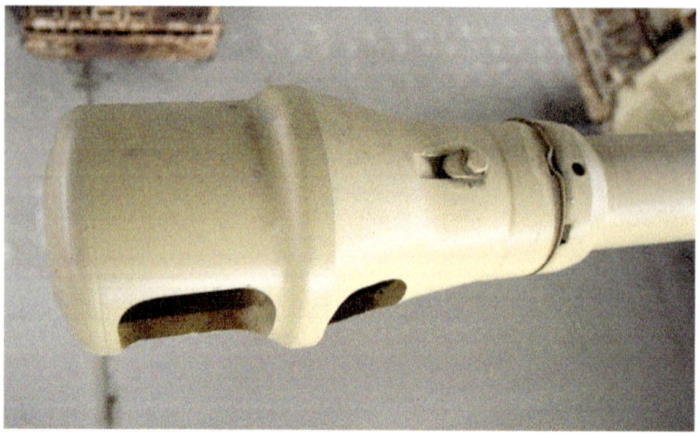

2

PANZER V AUSF. A PANTHER TANK AT FORT BENNING

In April 2019, this *Panzerkampfwagen* V *Ausführung* A tank was stored in the outside tank shelter along with other tanks waiting for its turn to be restored. The top of the tank is normally covered in a tarpaulin for additional protection. (© *U.S. Army Armor and Cavalry Collection*)

This Panther had the turret number 328 when captured; it belonged to the 3rd SS Panzer Regiment, 1st *Leibstandarte* SS Adolf Hitler (3/SS Pz. Rgt. 1 LSSAH). It was captured in St Barthelemy near Mortain, Normandy, after it was damaged by a mine. It was displayed for years at the former APG museum outside in a field, exposed to the elements.

The distant origins of the 1st SS-Panzer-Division *Leibstandarte* SS Adolf Hitler go back to the *Sturmabteilung* (SA) in early 1923. The initial recruits were responsible for guarding Adolf Hitler. They were his bodyguards at political rallies, meetings, and events. As the Nazis gained power, their numbers increased, and they took responsibility for guarding the *Führer*'s person, offices, and residences. They became the size of a regiment, but later, the LSSAH grew into an elite *Schutzstaffel* (SS) division. It was designated as a SS Panzer division in October 1943.

The *Leibstandarte* is a complicated word; it literally translates to 'body standard'. The nearest approximation to a British Army unit would be a regiment of guards like the Coldstream Guards or Irish Guards.

One major problem is when the APG assigned tracking numbers to the vehicles; it appears all the Panthers received the same number. Unfortunately, this FMVC number was later used to catalogue them into the museum system, so multiple vehicle records pop up under the same registration number.

THE PANZER AUSF. A PANTHER TANK DESIGN AND PRODUCTION

The *Ausführung* A was the second version of the Panther tank; the first was the *Ausführung* D. Many features of the Ausf. D (like the drum-shaped commander's cupola and the thin rectangular 'letterbox' hull machine gun port) were still present on early production Ausf. A Panthers produced between July to December 1943.

These only changed in mid-production and not at the same time. Other modifications were introduced during the production run. Ausf. D and Ausf. A tanks were also upgraded with different features once they had been issued to a Panzer division when they went to a maintenance or repair unit.

The long name for this tank was *Panzerkampfwagen* V 'Panther' (7.5-cm KwK L/70) (Sd.Kfz.171) *Ausführung* A. The hull used for the early production Panzer V Ausf. A was precisely the same as that used for the Ausf. D. These new Panther tanks were given a new version designation, Ausf. A, because they were fitted with an improved turret.

The tank hulls were produced at four different locations: Daimler-Benz produced Fgst.Nr. 151901 to 152575; *Maschinenfabrik* Niedersachsen Hannover (MNH) produced Fgst.Nr. 154801 to 155630; Demag-Benrath produced 158101 to 158150; and MAN produced 210255 to 210899.

THE TURRET

The new Ausf. A turret, like the hulls, underwent changes during its production. The 7.5-cm KwK 42 L/70 gun was the same, and so was the binocular TZF 12 gunsight. The external shape of the new turret looked very similar to the older Ausf. D turret, but there were some subtle changes. The gun mantlet on the Ausf. A turret was wider than the one fitted to the older Ausf. D. Directly behind the gun mantlet, the shape of the cast turret side had changed to a dish-shaped protrusion to fit the new seal for the gun mantlet.

On the older Ausf. D turret, the front and side armour plate used a dovetail-angled, carpentry-style welded joint. The new Ausf. A turret plates were welded together using an interlocking squared-off joint, with the top and bottom cut parallel to the turret base.

The loader had a periscope mounted in the turret roof. The *Rohrausblasevorrichtung* (powder gas extractor) for the gun was improved. The Ausf. D turret had a single-speed power traverse system. A new variable-speed unit was fitted to the Ausf. A. To prevent rainwater entering into the tank during fording, a new spring-compressed sealing ring was fitted to the turret ring.

Early production Ausf. A Panthers were fitted with the Ausf. D round drum-like commander's cupola. A new dome-shaped cast armour commander's cupola was gradually introduced. It had seven periscopes with armoured protective cowlings. It was fitted with a 1 o'clock to 12 o'clock azimuth indicator ring, which moved with the turret. The gunner also had a 1 o'clock to 12 o'clock azimuth indicator mounted to his left. This helped with target acquisition communication. The commander could shout, 'enemy tanks 7 o'clock', and the gunner would know where to look. On 1 August 1943, a ring was mounted on the commander's cupola to enable an anti-aircraft machine gun to be installed.

The early production Ausf. A turrets had three pistol ports: one on each side and one on the rear. To make production simpler and the armour stronger, the pistol ports were dropped from late-production Ausf. A turrets. Instead, a *Nahverteidgungswaffe* (close defence weapon) was fitted to the roof of the tank to the right of the commander's cupola. It could fire a high-explosive grenade in the direction of attacking infantry. The crew were safe from the shrapnel inside the tank, but enemy soldiers would be exposed. The *Nahverteidgungswaffe* could also be used to fire smoke grenades and signal flares. It looked like a large flare pistol.

The early production Ausf. A turrets had the same gunner's binocular TZF 12 gunsight with a rain guard over the two lenses that were fitted on the earlier Ausf. D turrets. This was changed to a monocular TZF 12a gunsight starting in late November 1943. There was now only one hole on the gunner's side at the front of the turret, not two. The design of the gun mantlet had to be changed to accommodate this new single-lens gunsight. A smaller semi-circular rain guard was added to the design.

These changes to the turret design were not introduced at the same time. There are photographs of Ausf. A turrets with the new commander's dome-shaped cupola, but the sides still had pistol ports and the binocular gunsight mounted in the gun mantlet.

BELLY AND DECK ARMOUR

The construction of the Panther Ausf. A hull belly armour was not consistent. Some hull belly armour was made from one sheet of 16-mm armour. Others were constructed in two parts with the front part being 30 mm thick to help cope with the damage caused by anti-tank mines. The third variation was formed of three separate armour plates. The front two were 30 mm thick, and the rear one was 16 mm thick. It is not known precisely when these changes were introduced or which factory followed which authorised plans.

The construction of the deck armour was also inconsistent. Some hull deck armour was built from a single piece of 16-mm armoured plate. Others were formed by welding three different pieces of 16-mm-thick armoured plate.

SIDE ARMOUR

The eight large double-interleaved, rubber-rimmed steel road-wheels positioned on either side of the hull provided more armoured protection for the thin, 40-mm-thick, surface-hardened hull sides than the smaller wheel used on the Panzer III and IV. The gap between the top of the wheels and the panniers was covered by plates of *Schürzen* designed to stop Soviet 14.5-mm anti-tank rifle rounds penetrating the 40-mm hull armour.

It is a common misconception that *Schürzen* decreased the effectiveness of a bazooka rocket. Those rounds went straight through the armour plates, leaving a clean round hole. The German *Waffenamt* (Weapons Agency) carried out tests in December 1944. They concluded that side skirt armour did not degrade the penetration of shaped-charge rockets. The US Army tested skirt armour in early January 1945 as a possible defence against German *Panzerfaust*- and *Panzerschreck*-shaped charges and also found they had no effect. They did not stop shaped charges; in fact, the distance between the skirt armour and the tank hull in many cases helped the formation of the armour-piercing jet.

HULL MACHINE GUN

Early production Ausf. A tanks had the same rectangular 'letterbox' pistol port in the front glacis plate, out of which the radio operator could fire a machine gun. In late November 1943, a *Kugelblende* (ball mount) with a spherical armoured guard was introduced. The radio operator could now see forward through the machine gunsight. The forward-facing periscope was no longer fitted. His side periscope was repositioned 25 mm further to the right.

SIDE STRAPS

Most metal straps for holding tools, spare parts, and stowage boxes were welded or bolted to the top of the hull or under the pannier, just above the track. Panthers built by Demag-Benrath were the exception. They welded the spare track hangers and base-bar directly to the side of the hull.

SUSPENSION

The Panzer V Ausf. A hull used the same dual torsion bar suspension system used on the earlier Ausf. D, but numerous changes were introduced during the production run at different times and locations. In August 1943, the road-wheels were strengthened with twenty-four outer rim bolts, but road-wheels with sixteen rim bolts were still being fitted to some Panthers in as late as March 1944. When new wheels were damaged, there would be a chance that they could be replaced with the older sixteen-rim-bolted wheels at the maintenance yard. Some had locking rectangular tabs on the inner face of the replacement production series road-wheels. The design of the armour casing for the final drive housing was altered during the production run of Ausf. A Panthers. The armoured hub cap that went over the centre of the drive sprocket was also changed midway through production. Not all Panzer V Ausf. A Panther tanks looked the same.

EXHAUST PIPES

The early production Panther Ausf. A had the same layout as on the Ausf. D tank with two vertical exhaust pipes sticking out of individual curved armoured guards at the rear of the tank. The red convoy light was fixed below the left pannier above the track.

Later, the left side pipe was altered. Two cooling pipes were added. Now, three long vertical pipes came out of a modified armoured curved cover. There was still only one exhaust pipe coming out of the armoured cover on the right side of the tank. The red convoy light was moved from over the left track to the immediate left side of the left exhaust armoured cover at the rear of the tank.

CAMOUFLAGE

In February 1943, all factories were instructed to paint all German armoured fighting vehicles *dunkelgelb* (RAL 7028 dark sandy yellow). Each Panzer unit then applied its own individual camouflage pattern. They were issued with *olivegrün* (RAL 6003 olive green) and *rotbraun* (RAL 8017 reddish brown) paint. In the winter, a covering of whitewash was applied to the tanks.

PRODUCTION

Four companies were involved in the assembly of the Panther Ausf. A: MAN produced Panther Ausf. A tanks with hull numbers Fgst.Nr. 210255–210899; Daimler-Benz produced Panther Ausf. A tanks with hull numbers Fgst.Nr. 151901–152575; MNH produced Panther Ausf. A tanks with hull numbers Fgst.Nr. 154801–155630; and Demag-Benrath produced Panther Ausf. A tanks with hull numbers Fgst.Nr. 158101–158150. The first Panther Ausf. A tanks were completed in August 1943. They did not take part in the Battle of Kursk, which began on 5 July 1943 and lasted until 23 August. The first Panther Ausf. A tanks arrived in Poland in September 1943.

PANTHER AUSF. A SPECIFICATIONS	
Dimensions (L-W-H)	8.86 m × 3.42 m × 3.10 m (29 feet 1 inch × 11 feet 3 inches × 10 feet 2 inches)
Total weight, battle-ready	45.5 tonnes
Main Armament	7.5-cm KwK 42 L/70, 79 rounds
Secondary Armament	2 × 7.92-mm MG 34 machine guns
Armour: front upper glacis	80 mm at 55 degrees
Armour: front lower hull	60 mm at 55 degrees
Armour: hull side	40 mm at 0 degrees
Armour: side superstructure	40 mm at 40 degrees
Armour: rear	40 mm at 30 degrees
Armour: hull deck	16 mm at 90 degrees
Armour: belly	30/16/16 mm (or all 16 mm) at 90 degrees
Armour: turret gun mantlet	100 mm at rounded
Armour: turret front	100 mm at 12 degrees
Armour: turret sides	45 mm at 25 degrees
Armour: turret rear	45 mm at 25 degrees
Armour: turret deck	16 mm at 84.5–90 degrees
Crew	5 (commander, driver, gunner, loader, radioman/machine gunner)
Propulsion	Maybach HL 230 P30 V12 water-cooled 700-hp petrol/gasoline engine
Max Road Speed	55 km/h (34 mph)
Transmission	ZF AK 7-200 7-forward/1-reverse gearbox
Suspension	Double torsion bars and interleaved wheels
Operational range	200 km (124 miles)
Production	2,200

The rear armour on the Panther Ausf. A was 40 mm thick and angled at 30 degrees. The side superstructure armour covering the internal stowage panniers was 40 mm thick and angled at 40 degrees. The side hull armour was also 40 mm thick but vertical. (© *U.S. Army Armor and Cavalry Collection*)

Some early MAN production Panther Ausf. A tank turrets still had the drum-shaped tank commander's cupola. Later produced turrets had cast dome-shaped cupolas as on this turret. The gun sighting vane can be seen at the front of the cupola; they were not present on early dome-shaped cast cupolas. Different features were added or changed throughout the Panther Ausf. A production run. Daimler-Benz and MNH do not seem to have been informed of the design change to fit the AA ring immediately at the start of production, leading to a few of their first Panther Ausf. A being accepted into service without a ring on the cast cupola. (© *U.S. Army Armor and Cavalry Collection*)

The front of the commander's cupola had a sighting vane, a gun laying tool that consisted of two triangles. The rear one had a 'V' cut into the top. When the tip of the front triangle was between the rear 'V', the commander could see where the tank's gun was pointing and whether it was facing the right target. (© *U.S. Army Armor and Cavalry Collection*)

MNH was the first plant to start Panther Ausf. A production; they assembled theirs immediately with the cast cupola, as did Daimler-Benz. The MAN factory was the only one to have had a limited initial run of Ausf. A with the drum cupola. The cast armour dome-shaped cupola body was inset with seven periscopes that were protected by armoured cowlings. (© *U.S. Army Armor and Cavalry Collection*)

Starting from 1 August 1943, factories were instructed to fit an anti-aircraft machine gun mounting ring to the top of the commander's cupola. The anti-aircraft machine gun mounting ring was already being installed on some late production Ausf. D drum cupolas, so it was not a new fitting only mounted on the new Ausf. A turret. However, both MNH and Daimler-Benz finished their initial Ausf. A turrets without the ring. The *Fliegerbeschussgerät* 7.92-mm MG 34 machine gun mount was fixed on top of the ring. (© *U.S. Army Armor and Cavalry Collection*)

A periscope was added to the roof for the main gun loader. It had an armoured cover. This was a new feature introduced on the Panzer V Ausf. A turret. (© *U.S. Army Armor and Cavalry Collection*)

This is the armoured cover for the turret deck's *Rohrausblasevorrichtung* (powder gas extractor fan). When the main gun or the coaxial machine gun was fired, noxious fumes built up and needed to be extracted. The vents that face forward and to the side are protected by a semi-circular welded armoured guard. This turret ventilator cover is of the welded type, which indicates the turret came from Eisenwerke Oberdonau. (© *U.S. Army Armor and Cavalry Collection*)

This is the front view of the Panther Ausf. A turret deck's *Rohrausblasevorrichtung* and armoured cover with its semi-circular armoured guard. Behind it is the loader's periscope opening and its armoured guard. (© *U.S. Army Armor and Cavalry Collection*)

The Panther Ausf. A turrets did not have these J-shaped brackets welded to the turret roof when they left the factory. They were battlefield modifications used to hang additional tank track links to the side of the turret and not fitted in the factory. They were called *Ersatzkettengliederhalterung* (*ersatz* = spare, *ketten* = chain, *glieder* = links, but *kettenglieder* = tracks, *halterung* = holder). This would give added armour protection to the crew and enable them to deal with broken tracks due to mine damage. (© *U.S. Army Armor and Cavalry Collection*)

Additional tank track links are hung on the side of this restored Panzer V Ausf. A Panther turret in France using the J-shaped brackets welded to the turret roof.

The early production Panther Ausf. A turrets had a pistol port to the left of the large circular hatch at the rear of the turret. Turrets completed in February 1944 did not have the pistol port as in this example. On turrets completed from June 1944 onwards, a handle was fitted on the middle of the rear circular hatch. These features date this turret being produced between February and May 1944. By July 1944, MNH had the last factory still assembling the Ausf. A, with only eleven completed before switching to Ausf. G production. (© *U.S. Army Armor and Cavalry Collection*)

The Panther Ausf. D and early Ausf. A turrets had a pistol port in the turret side and rear armour. To simplify and speed up production, these were not included in mid-production Panther Ausf. A turrets starting from December 1943. They were also considered a weak point in the turrets armour. In March 1944, a *Nahverteidigungswaffe* was installed into the turret deck that launched shrapnel grenades, which would kill any enemy soldiers near the tank. Panther turrets like this one, built between December 1943 and March 1944, did not have any additional close protection weapons other than the coaxial machine gun. This situation arose because of delays in the supply of the *Nahverteidigungswaffe* reaching the assembly factories. (© *U.S. Army Armor and Cavalry Collection*)

This turret was not fitted with a side pistol port or *Nahverteidigungswaffe* (smoke and grenade discharger). In June 1943, following battlefield reports of smoke grenades exploding and releasing smoke around the tank after being hit by small arms fire, choking the crew and obscuring their vision of enemy targets, the smoke grenade dischargers were no longer fitted to Panther turrets. (© *U.S. Army Armor and Cavalry Collection*)

Just below the J-shaped spare track bracket is a long oval-shaped cut in the turret side armour. This is the mortise hole into which the tenon cut of the rear turret armour plate fits before being welded in place. (© *U.S. Army Armor and Cavalry Collection*)

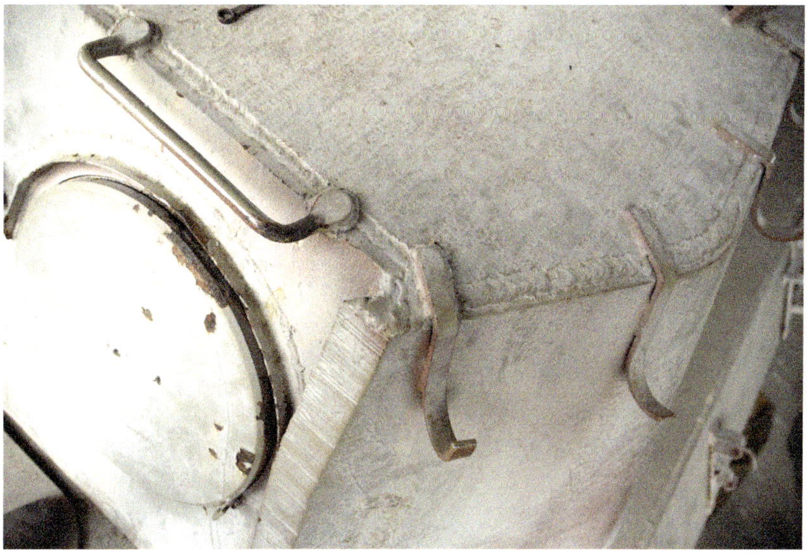

Late-production Panther Ausf. A rear turret hatches were fitted with a second handle in the middle of the hatch. Early and middle production turrets only had the handle above the hatch to help the crew get in and out of the hatch. This turret does not have the second handle fitted on the rear hatch. (© *U.S. Army Armor and Cavalry Collection*)

On late-production Panther Ausf. A turret decks, there would have been a large circular aperture behind the loader's periscope for the *Nahverteidigungswaffe*. Turrets with holes cut into the roof for the *Nahverteidigungswaffe* were being delivered by the forging plants starting November–December 1943. However, there were shortages of *Nahverteidigungswaffe* weapons, resulting in many Panther Ausf. A turrets having a circular plate bolted over the hole. They started to be fitted to Panther Ausf. A turrets after March 1944 as supplies reached the assembly factories. This turret is a rarity as it does not have any pistol ports, external smoke grenade launchers, a circular plate bolted over the hole in the turret deck, or a *Nahverteidigungswaffe* fitted. (© *U.S. Army Armor and Cavalry Collection*)

One of the differences between the earlier Ausf. D turret and this later Ausf. A turret is the way the interlocking side armour plates were welded with the front turret casting. The Ausf. A plates had a rectangular cut joint rather than a dovetail cut. There were a few early exceptions. Some turrets still had the dovetailed version, but the joints were covered with a *Zimmerit* (anti-magnetic mine paste) coating so are difficult to see in period photographs. (© *U.S. Army Armor and Cavalry Collection*)

The tool stowage rack was fitted to the right side of the superstructure side. It was used to attach the 450-mm C-Hook, wire cutters, fire extinguisher, starter crank, wooden block for the jack, track tensioning tool, sledgehammer and the cable used for replacing track. (© *U.S. Army Armor and Cavalry Collection*)

On the top of the commander's cupola, a ring for the anti-aircraft machine gun mount was added to Panther Ausf. A turrets starting from 1 August 1943. (© *U.S. Army Armor and Cavalry Collection*)

The 100-mm-thick gun mantlet was more curved than that fitted to the gun on the earlier Ausf. D turret. It was delivered to the gun assembly factory to be mounted on the finished gun. Both were then transported to the tank assembly factory. (© *U.S. Army Armor and Cavalry Collection*)

Panther Ausf. D and early Ausf. A turrets were fitted with a binocular TZF 12 gunsight. These could be identified by two holes side by side visible to the left side of the main gun in the mantlet. Starting in late November–early December 1943, these were replaced by monocular TZF 12a gunsights as fitted to this tank turret. The single hole in the gun mantlet had a semi-circular rain guard over it. (© *U.S. Army Armor and Cavalry Collection*)

Aperture for the coaxial 7.92-mm MG 34 machine gun. (© *U.S. Army Armor and Cavalry Collection*)

This turret does not have the long thin rain and debris guard metal strip that would cover the gap between the gun mantlet and the turret. (© *U.S. Army Armor and Cavalry Collection*)

This inverted U-shaped lug on top of the turret deck was used for lifting the turret off the hull. (© *U.S. Army Armor and Cavalry Collection*)

The driver had a forward- and sideways-looking periscope poking out of the hull deck protected by their own armoured covers. (© *U.S. Army Armor and Cavalry Collection*)

On this side view, the driver's hatch, forward- and sideways-looking periscopes, and armoured vent cover under the gun lock base are visible. (© *U.S. Army Armor and Cavalry Collection*)

When the front glacis plate machine gun ball mount was added to the tank, the radio operator/bow machine gunner could now look forward through the machine gun mount. The forward-looking, roof-mounted periscope was removed. The remaining side vision periscope fitted to the Panther Ausf. A was moved 25 mm further to the right from its previous location on the Ausf. D. When the hatch was opened, it raised up to clear the periscope's armoured cover. (© *U.S. Army Armor and Cavalry Collection*)

This is the lock to prevent the radio operator/bow machine gunner's hatch lid from swinging shut and causing injury to the crewman. (© *U.S. Army Armor and Cavalry Collection*)

Front view of the radio operator/bow machine gunner's hatch lock for when it was in the open position. (© *U.S. Army Armor and Cavalry Collection*)

The radio operator/bow machine gunner's hatch lock for when it was in the closed position. (© *U.S. Army Armor and Cavalry Collection*)

Above left: Gun travel lock. (© *U.S. Army Armor and Cavalry Collection*)

Above right: The gun travel lock fitted over the 323-mm-diameter armoured cap for the front hull vent. (© *U.S. Army Armor and Cavalry Collection*)

Right: The Panther Ausf. D and early production Panther Ausf. A hulls still had the 'letterbox' machine gun opening in the glacis plate. Starting late November–early December 1943, it was replaced by a ball mount for the hull 7.92-mm MG 34 machine gun. (© *U.S. Army Armor and Cavalry Collection*)

The 7.92-mm MG 34 hull machine gun ball mount was protected by a spherical armoured guard. To prevent bullet splinters flying up the glacis plate and jamming the ball mount, two ridges were built into the bottom of the guard. (© *U.S. Army Armor and Cavalry Collection*)

Panther Ausf. A hulls just like the earlier Ausf. D hulls still had driver's vision ports in the front glacis plate protected by a rectangular armoured hatch. They had a forward- and sideways-looking periscope poking out of the hull deck protected by their own armoured covers. (© *U.S. Army Armor and Cavalry Collection*)

The early production Panther Ausf. D hulls had two Bosch *Tarnlampe* bolted to the front glacis plate, one on each side. Starting from September 1943, only one headlight, with blackout cover, was fitted to the left side of the tank. The Ausf. A tank hulls also only had one headlight bolted to the glacis plate on the left side. This is the headlight mount. The headlight is missing. (© *U.S. Army Armor and Cavalry Collection*)

This is the front view of the Bosch *Tarnlampe* mount. The headlight is missing. The hole in front of the mount in the glacis plate was for the electric cable. (© *U.S. Army Armor and Cavalry Collection*)

Side view of the Bosch *Tarnlampe* mount. You can also see the 80-mm-thick glacis plate interlocking squared-off welded joints with the 40-mm-thick side superstructure armour. A shell hitting the front angled glacis plate at 'normal' (0 degrees), would have to penetrate around 138 mm of armour. The vertical armour of a Tiger I tank was only 100 mm thick. (© *U.S. Army Armor and Cavalry Collection*)

Over the Panther Ausf. A production run, there were four major alterations to the layout of the rear of the tank. This layout was the third in that series. The left exhaust pipe had twin pipes mounted parallel and either side of it. These were used for the engine manifold cooling system. They are missing. (© *U.S. Army Armor and Cavalry Collection*)

The large circular disk between the two armour guards for the exhaust pipes is the engine access hatch. Just under the right-side exhaust pipe armoured cover, a guide for the hand crank used to turn the inertia starter was bolted into position. This was a new feature introduced in the third version of layout alterations at the rear of the Panther Ausf. A tank. (© *U.S. Army Armor and Cavalry Collection*)

This large hole on the left of the armoured exhaust cover is for the left side twin pipe mounted parallel and either side of the central exhaust pipe. The twin pipes were used for the engine manifold cooling system. They are both missing. (© *U.S. Army Armor and Cavalry Collection*)

Two mounting brackets for the 20-tonne jack were welded onto the rear hull between the two exhaust pipes. This was a new feature introduced in the third version of layout alterations at the rear of the Panther Ausf. A tank. (© *U.S. Army Armor and Cavalry Collection*)

Larger stowage bins would have been fixed to the rear armour plate in this location just above the track on both sides of the vehicle. They are missing. (© *U.S. Army Armor and Cavalry Collection*)

The hook at the rear of the tank on the upper section of the rear superstructure armour was used to attach lifting chains when the hull was being moved in the factory by a crane, lifted onto a recovery vehicle or ship. (© *U.S. Army Armor and Cavalry Collection*)

The eyelets at the rear of the tank were normally fitted with a U-shaped bracket and bolt. They had many uses: in the factory, they were used to lift the hull up using cranes or chain pullies; they could also be used to attach tow cables and for attaching securing cables when being transported by ship or train. (© *U.S. Army Armor and Cavalry Collection*)

Rear right-side rectangular engine-cooling air-intake vent on the engine deck next to the circular armoured guard and mesh cover over the engine air exhaust fan. The protective armour casing and mesh is missing. There were four of these vents built into the engine deck. (© *U.S. Army Armor and Cavalry Collection*)

Forward right-side rectangular engine-cooling air-intake vent armoured guard and mesh cover on the engine deck. (© *U.S. Army Armor and Cavalry Collection*)

Forward and rear left-side rectangular engine-cooling air-intake vents on the engine deck. The rear one is missing its armoured guard and mesh cover. The two circular armoured caps with handles are for the engine air-intake holes. (© *U.S. Army Armor and Cavalry Collection*)

Rear left side rectangular engine-cooling air-intake vents on the engine deck. It is missing its armoured guard and mesh cover. (© *U.S. Army Armor and Cavalry Collection*)

Rear right-side rectangular engine-cooling air-intake vents on the engine deck. It is missing its armoured guard and mesh cover. (© *U.S. Army Armor and Cavalry Collection*)

At the rear of the engine deck, there are three circular caps: from bottom to top, they are the rain guard for the fuel-filler cap, air-intake hole (where a deep-water fording snorkel tube could be fitted), and the coolant-filler cap. The two circular armoured caps with handles are for the engine air-intake holes. (© *U.S. Army Armor and Cavalry Collection*)

The cylindrical stowage bin on the left superstructure side was used to house the gun-cleaning brushes, rods, and spare antenna rods. The end caps were held in place by clips and a chain retainer. The support straps were welded to the superstructure side. (© *U.S. Army Armor and Cavalry Collection*)

The stowage frames were welded to the side of the superstructure rather than being bolted as this would have weakened the armour. (© *U.S. Army Armor and Cavalry Collection*)

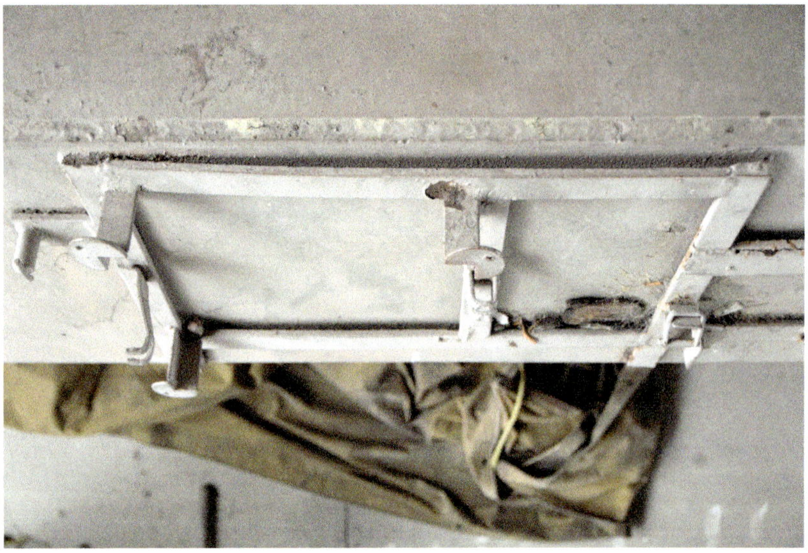

The rectangular frame on the right superstructure side was used for holding the wooden block for the jack. (© *U.S. Army Armor and Cavalry Collection*)

The wedge-shaped side armour plate gave added volume inside the Panther, so a larger fuel tank could be mounted on both sides of the tank. Sloping fuel tanks assisted drainage. (© *U.S. Army Armor and Cavalry Collection*)

Spare tank tracks could be strapped to the side of the tank hull at the rear and on the side of the turret. These have been applied to this restored Panzer V Ausf. A Panther tank in the Museum of Armour in Saumur. You can also see the rear stowage box and *Schürzen*.

A frame was welded to the superstructure side armour and bolted to the engine deck. Spare tank tracks were strapped to the side of the Panther Ausf. A superstructure at the rear along the length of the engine deck as well as on J-shaped brackets attached to the turret roof. (© *U.S. Army Armor and Cavalry Collection*)

Rear engine deck armoured air-intake and exhaust guards with mesh screens. (© *U.S. Army Armor and Cavalry Collection*)

The vertical straps of the spare track hanger frame were welded to the side armour so as not to weaken it and bolted to the thin hull deck. (© *U.S. Army Armor and Cavalry Collection*)

Vertical straps of the spare track hanger frame nearer to the turret. (© *U.S. Army Armor and Cavalry Collection*)

Female bracket for the *Schürzen* hanger welded onto the bottom of the Panther tank's left-hand pannier at the rear. (© *U.S. Army Armor and Cavalry Collection*)

Female bracket for the *Schürzen* hanger welded onto the bottom of the Panther tank's left-hand pannier in the middle. (© *U.S. Army Armor and Cavalry Collection*)

The Panther tank's suspension system consisted of a front-drive sprocket wheel that powered the track, a rear idler wheel, and eight large double-interleaved rubber-rimmed steel road-wheels on either side of the hull. The rubber is missing from some of these road-wheels. (© *U.S. Army Armor and Cavalry Collection*)

The Panther's suspension system was not easy to repair. When the torsion bars were damaged, it sometimes needed a welder's torch to cut them out. (© *U.S. Army Armor and Cavalry Collection*)

This Panther Ausf. A hull was fitted with a front-drive sprocket ring that had thirty-two (not sixteen bolts as found on the Ausf. D and some earlier Ausf. A versions) countersunk rim bolts with crowned heads held by cotter pins. (© *U.S. Army Armor and Cavalry Collection*)

The strengthened idler wheel had 15-mm-wide spokes. (© *U.S. Army Armor and Cavalry Collection*)

Starting in August 1943, reinforced inner and outer road-wheels with twenty-four rim bolts were introduced. The earlier version of tank road-wheels used on the Panther Ausf. D only had sixteen rim bolts. The large interleaved road-wheels caused problems for the crew when they had to replace a damaged internal wheel. They had to unbolt several wheels to get at the broken one. This was time-consuming. Ice, mud and rocks could clog the interleaved wheels. In the severe winter weather on the Eastern Front, they could freeze solid overnight. (© *U.S. Army Armor and Cavalry Collection*)

On the side of the Panther hull, you can see a track pin return plate, a bump in the side of the wall. If a track pin came loose on the earlier Panther Ausf. D version of the tank, it was found to cause minor but significant damage that could disable the vehicle. The solution was to weld a track pin return plate onto the side of the hull. This specific heart-shaped pin return plate was a short-lived design; it was replaced by the much simpler to produce rectangular bent plate. (© *U.S. Army Armor and Cavalry Collection*)

The outside exposed end of the track pin was kept in place by a 40-mm-diameter retainer ring held by a split pin. (© *U.S. Army Armor and Cavalry Collection*)

This is not the track used on the Panther Ausf. A. It comes from a Jagdtiger, but you can see the circular flat end of the track pin that would be nearest to the hull armour. These pins are similar to those used on the Panther. The outside exposed end of the track pin was kept in place by a 40-mm-diameter retainer ring held by a split pin. If this came loose, then the inner flat end of the track pin would be knocked back into position by the track pin return plate, a bump in the side of the hull wall. (© *U.S. Army Armor and Cavalry Collection*)

The Panther tank's tracks were called Kgs 64/660/150 (code for fast running track for motor vehicles made, steel castings of all alloys, with rotating bolts, type 64, width 660 mm, spacing 150 mm). (© *U.S. Army Armor and Cavalry Collection*)

View of the bottom of the pannier and top of the track on the left side of the Panther Ausf. A tank. (© *U.S. Army Armor and Cavalry Collection*)

The lower curved section of the track guard is missing on this Panther Ausf. A. (© *U.S. Army Armor and Cavalry Collection*)

3

PANZER V AUSF. G PANTHER TRAINING TANK AT FORT BENNING

This Panzer V Ausf. G Panther tank looks relatively intact when viewed from its right side. (© *U.S. Army Armor and Cavalry Collection*)

This is a late-production Panzer V Ausf. G Panther tank. It is fitted with a 'chin guard' on the gun mantlet. It was recovered in Europe and shipped to America. At present, no further operational history has been discovered about this tank. The side armour was cut away to enable it to be used as an educational training tank for US Army tank crews. It was on display at the Aberdeen Proving Ground in Maryland for many years before being transported to the US Army Armour and Cavalry Collection at Fort Benning in Georgia.

THE PANZER AUSF. G PANTHER TANK DESIGN AND PRODUCTION

The Panzer V Panther tank was given the Ausf. G version designation to indicate that this production run of tanks used a different, redesigned hull. The turret and 7.5-cm KwK L/70 tank gun were the same ones used on the earlier Ausf. A.

On 4 May 1944, during a meeting at the MAN company, a decision was made to design a new Panther tank hull. Work had started on developing a new version of the Panther tank, with thicker armour, called the Panther II, but that was far from completion. Some of the lessons learnt from that design process were used in formulating the plans for the Ausf. G tank hull.

The side pannier armour that covered the top of the tracks on both sides of the tank was angled at 40 degrees on the Ausf. D and Ausf. A tank hull. The new hull pannier side armour was sloped at 29 degrees. The thickness of the armour was increased from 40 to 50 mm. This increased the weight of the tank by 305 kg.

To compensate for this increase in weight, the designers looked for areas where the thickness of the armour could be reduced. They chose to use 50-mm armour plating on the lower front hull instead of the standard 60 mm. This saved 150 kg. The forward belly plates were reduced to 25 mm from 30 mm. The front two belly plates were 25 mm thick, and the rear plate was 16 mm thick. This saved a further 100 kg in weight. The rear side armour wedges at the end of the superstructure were not part of the new design. The floor of the pannier was now a straight line. These weight reduction changes meant that the increase inside armour thickness did not result in an increase in weight of the Ausf. G tank hull compared with the older hulls.

As the bottom of the pannier was now 50 mm nearer to the top of the track, no weld seams or stowage straps were fixed there. This was to stop them coming into contact with the track as the tank drove fast over undulating ground. Instead, the stowage straps were welded to the side of the pannier armour.

There were many other minor changes, but the overall thinking behind the design was to simplify the construction process to enable more tanks to be built as fast as possible. For example, the ventilation systems for the transmission, brakes, engine, and exhaust were redesigned. This meant that the two additional parallel vertical pipes that came out of the left armoured exhaust cover at the rear of the tank on the late production Ausf. A tank hull were no longer needed.

Starting in May 1944, cast armour exhaust guards gradually replaced welded ones. To help reduce the red glow given off by the exhaust pipes at night, as a temporary solution, sheet metal covers were gradually introduced starting in June 1944. Beginning in October 1944, these were progressively replaced with purpose-built *Flammenvernichter* (flame-suppressor exhaust mufflers). When additional supplies became available, they were back-fitted to other Panther tanks.

Another simplification of the production process was to introduce less complicated hinged hatches above the heads of the driver and radio operator. It was found during trials that the performance of the cross-country ride of the tank with or without the rear shock absorber was practically the same. Starting from 7 October 1944, the factories were ordered to stop fitting them to help simplify production.

THE DRIVER'S POSITION

A perceived weak spot was the driver's armoured vision port cut into the front glacis plate. This was deleted in the design of the Ausf. G hull. The driver was provided with a single pivoting traversable periscope, mounted in the roof of the hull covered by an armoured rain shield. Starting in August 1944, it was covered by a larger hood rain shield. This change in design helped simplify construction. When building the older Ausf. A hulls, three features had to be built—the driver's armoured vision port plus the forward and side periscopes. Now, only one periscope had to be fitted.

SIDE SKIRT ARMOUR AND HEADLIGHT

When looking at the side of the Panther Ausf. G hull, it appears that the track guard is jutting out of the steeper-angled pannier side armour along the whole length of the tank. This is an optical illusion. It is a fender, introduced on this hull, to enable the *Schürzen* to be hung in the correct position. They were designed to protect the thinner 40-mm hull side armour, visible above the top of the road-wheels and under the pannier, from Soviet anti-tank rifles. It meets the front track fender.

The single headlight on the Ausf. A hull was mounted on the left side of the upper glacis plate. To make fitting the headlight easier, it was moved to the top of the left front track guard on the Ausf. G hulls.

AMMUNITION STOWAGE AND MACHINE GUN BALL MOUNT

Two 4-mm-thick dust-cover sliding doors were introduced to close off the sponson ammunition racks. Starting in September 1944, these were no longer installed as it was found they got in the way of ammunition handling. The ammunition stowage area was changed so the tank could now carry eighty-two 7.5-cm main gun rounds.

There was now a distinct 'step' around the bottom of the late production Ausf. G 7.92-mm MG 34 machine gun ball mount armoured cover. This was to reduce enemy bullet splash entering the mount's aperture. The machine gun ball mount was considered a weak spot by enemy infantry and was often targeted. If a bullet hit the sloped glacis plate below the mount, it would ricochet upwards. The 'step' helped reduce the damage they could do.

RADIO

Most Panther Ausf. G tanks were fitted with a FuG 5 radio set and an internal intercom. It had a usable range of around 4–6 km depending on the atmospheric conditions and location of the tank. Hills reduced the radio's range. Platoon leaders and company HQ tanks were fitted with an additional FuG 2 radio for a command channel.

PRODUCTION

On 3 April 1944, MAN reported that it had successfully completed trial production runs of the new Ausf. G hull. MAN built about 1,143 Panther Ausf. G tanks between March 1944 and April 1945. Between July 1944 to March 1945, MNH constructed 806 Panther Ausf. G tanks. Daimler-Benz finished 1,004 Panther Ausf. G tanks between May 1944 and April 1945.

There were some minor differences between factory-built tanks. MNH fitted a cast steel *Gleitschuh* (skid shoe) instead of a rubber-rimmed return roller behind the front track drive sprocket. The other two factories continued to fit rubber-rimmed return rollers.

Starting in September 1944, MAN replaced the road-wheels on a few Panther Ausf. G tanks with smaller 800-mm-diameter steel tyre, rubber cushioned, road-wheels similar to the ones used on all Tiger II tanks and some Tiger I tanks. Although this saved on the amount of rubber required to build a new Panther tank, it had the disadvantage of reducing the vehicle's ground clearance by 30 mm. The slightly larger rubber rimmed tyres were 860-mm-diameter wheels. A few tanks built in April 1945 had rubber-rimmed road-wheels except for the one next to the idler wheel at the rear of the turret. That was fitted with a smaller steel tyre road-wheel. It is not known why.

Starting in October 1944, a larger-diameter self-cleaning idler wheel was fitted. This new idler wheel was introduced to help elevate the problems caused by the build-up of mud and ice. During the production run, some of the components of the suspension system changed like the swing arms and bump stops.

TURRET

A few minor changes were made to the turret during the production run. The most visible was the introduction of a handle on the circular hatch at the rear of the turret as well as the one above it. A thin rectangular metal sheet was welded across the gap between the front of the turret and the top of the gun mantlet to help stop debris entering the gap and jamming the gun elevation.

A lengthened rain guard over the gunsight aperture was added starting in September 1944. At the same time, a new gun mantlet was gradually introduced. It had a 'chin guard' to stop enemy armour-piercing shells ricocheting off the bottom of the mantlet, penetrating the roof of the hull, and entering the crew compartment. When Allied troops inspected the MNH Panther production factory at the end of the war, they found turrets were still being produced with the older curved gun mantlet without the 'chin guard'.

Starting in January 1945, five metal loops were welded to each turret side. Rope or wire was run between these loops to help hold in place branches from trees and bushes used as camouflage.

INFRARED SEARCHLIGHT AND SCOPE

To be able to see the enemy at night was a tank commander's dream. To be able to point the tank's gun at a target with the correct elevation as well was cutting edge technology in late 1944.

Starting in September 1944, a few Panzer V Ausf. G Panther tanks had a F.G.1250 *Ziel und Kommandanten-Optic für* Panther infrared searchlight and scope mounted on the commander's cupola. When the tank commander moved the scope up and down, an attached steel band, which had been fed through a hole in the turret roof, connected with a new indicator that showed the gunner the correct elevation. The 200-watt screened infrared light and receiver gunsight optic had a range of 600 m in clear weather.

It is not known precisely how many Panther tanks were fitted with this device or used on the battlefield. On 5 October 1944, MNH reported that it had equipped twenty Panther tanks with the new infrared equipment during September. Another thirty were scheduled to be completed in October with a further thirty in December 1944. On 15 January 1945, MNH were instructed to fit them to their entire current order for Panther Ausf. G tanks. It cannot be confirmed if this was done.

CAMOUFLAGE

Early production Panther Ausf. G tanks were delivered to the front line painted in *dunkelgelb* (RAL 7028 dark sandy yellow) on top of the *Zimmerit* (anti-magnetic mine paste) coating. Each Panzer unit then applied their own camouflage design. On 19 August 1944, an order was issued to the factories that the tanks should be painted in a new camouflage pattern known as 'Ambush'. Patches of *rotbraun* (RAL 8017 reddish brown) and *olivgrün* (olive green) were spray-painted over the *dunkelgelb* base coat.

Due to Allied and Soviet air supremacy in the later part of the war, Panther tank crews tried, where possible, to hide their tanks under tree. Dots of *dunkelgelb* were applied to the olive-green and reddy-brown patches to simulate light coming through a tree canopy. Darker dots were applied to the *dunkelgelb* base coat.

On 9 September 1944, because of reports that *Zimmerit* (anti-magnetic mine paste) had caused tank fires, and the lack of evidence of magnetic mine use by the Soviets and Allies, the factories were ordered to stop applying *Zimmerit*. Panther Ausf. G tanks now left the factory painted in a base coat of red oxide primer. They were only sparingly painted in camouflage patterns using *dunkelgelb* in patches. Paint supplies were getting low, and the need to get as many tanks to the front line as fast as possible was urgent.

On 31 October 1944, additional instructions were received at the factories. The inside of the Panther Ausf. G tanks were no longer to be painted *elfenbein* (a light ivory white colour). To save time, they were only painted in red oxide primer. This would make the inside of the tank a very dark working environment. The outside could be sparingly painted in patches of *rotbraun*, *dunkelgelb*, and *olivgrün*. If supplies of *dunkelgelb* ran out, the factories were authorised to use *dunkelgrau* (RAL 7021 dark grey) instead. On 15 February 1945, the factories were ordered to paint the inside of the turrets *elfenbein* again.

PANTHER AUSF. G SPECIFICATIONS	
Dimensions (L-W-H)	8.86 m × 3.42 m × 3.10 m (29 feet 1 inch × 11 feet 3 inches × 10 feet 2 inches)
Total weight, battle-ready	45.5 tonnes
Main Armament	7.5-cm KwK 42 L/70, 82 rounds
Secondary Armament	2 × 7.92-mm MG 34 machine guns
Armour: front upper glacis	80 mm at 55 degrees
Armour: front lower hull	50 mm at 55 degrees
Armour: hull side	40 mm at 0 degrees
Armour: side superstructure	50 mm at 29 degrees
Armour: rear	30 mm at 30 degrees
Armour: hull deck	40-16 mm at 90 degrees
Armour: belly	25-16 mm at 90 degrees
Armour: turret gun mantlet	100–110 mm at rounded
Armour: turret front	100 mm at 12 degrees
Armour: turret sides	45 mm at 25 degrees
Armour: turret rear	45 mm at 25 degrees
Armour: turret deck	16 mm at 84.5–90 degrees
Crew	5 (commander, driver, gunner, loader, radioman/machine gunner)
Propulsion	Maybach HL 230 P30 V12 water-cooled 600-hp petrol/gasoline engine
Transmission	ZF AK 7-200 7-forward/1-reverse gearbox
Suspension	Double torsion bars and interleaved wheels
Max Road Speed	46 km/h (28.5 mph)
Operational range	200 km (124 miles)
Production	2,961 approx.

TOTAL PRODUCTION NUMBERS

The number of Panzer V Panther tanks produced was recorded by hull number (Fgst.Nr.) for each *Ausführung* (version) and from factory monthly completion figures. The factory completion figures did not record the *Ausführung* information. Panther tank production occurred at factories belonging to the following companies: MAN, Daimler-Benz, MNH, and Henschel. A few were built by Demag. As you can see, the figures do not match.

Total Number Produced Using Hull Number Data (Fgst.Nr.)

Panzer V 'Panther' Ausf. D (Sd.Kfz.171) total	842
Panzer V 'Panther' Ausf. A (Sd.Kfz.171) total	2,200
Panzer V 'Panther' Ausf. G (Sd.Kfz.171) approx. total	2961
Grand total:	6,003

TOTAL PRODUCED USING MONTHLY FACTORY COMPLETION DATA

1943 total	1768
1944 total	3777
1945 total	439
Grand total	5,984

The left side has big chunks of armour cut away to expose the internal fighting compartment. This was done to enable it to be used as a training tool. It still serves that function today. Notice the gun mantlet has a 'chin guard'. (© *U.S. Army Armor and Cavalry Collection*)

The side armour of the rear engine compartment was not cut away. (© *U.S. Army Armor and Cavalry Collection*)

To assist in teaching new tank crews about the benefits of sloped armour on Second World War tanks, this Panther has details about the front glacis plate armour marked on the vehicle in black pen. (© *U.S. Army Armor and Cavalry Collection*)

The Panther's front glacis plate has been measured at a right angle to the face as being 85 mm (3.35 inches thick); 5 mm of that measurement appears to include the weld. (© *U.S. Army Armor and Cavalry Collection*)

The Panther's front glacis plate has been measured at 54 degrees to the face. Although the armour is only 80 mm thick, if an armour-piercing shell hit the sloped glacis plate at 54 degrees, it would have to penetrate 137–140 mm (5.375 inches) of armour. (© *U.S. Army Armor and Cavalry Collection*)

There are also measurements on the cut-out section of the upper hull superstructure side armour that is above the tank tracks. The armour thickness has been measured at 53 mm (2.1 inches). The additional 3 mm could be made up of paint layers. The armour is slopped at an angle of 29 degrees. An armour-piercing shell hitting this sloped armour plate at normal (a head-on attack at 90 degrees) would have to penetrate 57–60 mm (2.375 inches) of armour, not 50 mm. (© *U.S. Army Armor and Cavalry Collection*)

The front upper glacis plate and the side superstructure armour plate were welded together using interlocking rectangular joints to increase the strength of the junction. (© *U.S. Army Armor and Cavalry Collection*)

The hole in the side armour at the front of the Panther tank was used when the tank was lifted or towed. (© *U.S. Army Armor and Cavalry Collection*)

The front glacis plate and lower hull armour plate were also welded together using interlocking rectangular joints to increase the strength of the intersection. (© *U.S. Army Armor and Cavalry Collection*)

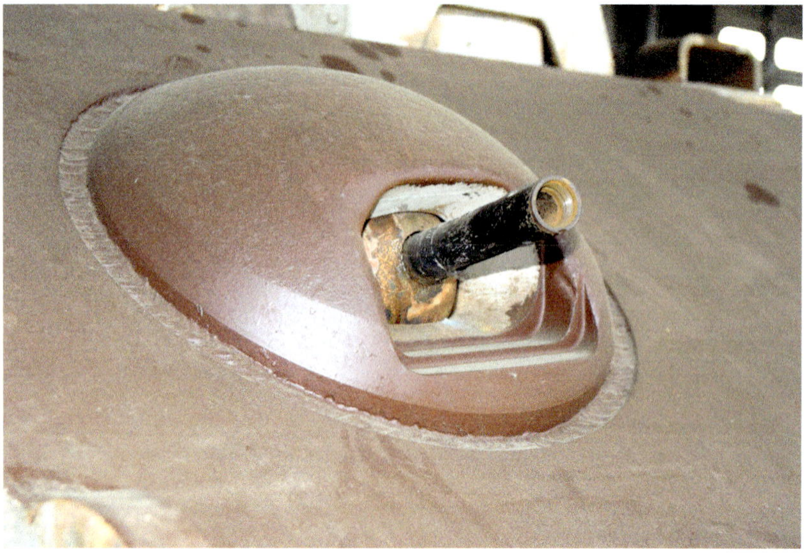

The Panzer V Ausf. G Panther tank hull was fitted with a 7.92-mm MG 34 machine gun in a cast armoured guard around a ball mount. There is a thick lip around the bottom of the mount. This was to reduce enemy bullet splash entering the mount's aperture, having first hit the sloped glacis plate below the mount and ricocheted upwards. (© *U.S. Army Armor and Cavalry Collection*)

The hull machine gunner could see forward through the 7.92-mm MG 34 machine gunsight. He had a rooftop armour-protected periscope that could provide vision to the right of the tank at the front. (© *U.S. Army Armor and Cavalry Collection*)

This is the gun travel lock in the down position. When the Panther was being transported or driving long distances in non-combat areas, the long gun barrel would be locked into the forward position to prevent it from being damaged. The gun travel lock is resting on the hull cabin vent's armoured cover. There was also an internal breech-locking mechanism inside the turret. (© *U.S. Army Armor and Cavalry Collection*)

The driver's periscope could swivel to give him better vision. It had an armoured cover. (© *U.S. Army Armor and Cavalry Collection*)

This is the front hull deck. The driver's hutch is in the foreground. It is missing the armoured hatch. In front of it is the driver's armoured cover for the swivelling periscope. Next to it in the middle is the gun travel lock over the hull cabin vent armoured cover. On the far side, there is the hull machine gunner's hatch and fixed periscope armoured cover. Both periscopes are missing. In case of an emergency exit, the hatches of the Ausf. G could be jettisoned away. (© *U.S. Army Armor and Cavalry Collection*)

There are a lot of features missing from the rear of this Panzer V Ausf. G Panther tank. The two brackets at the top of the armour plate were used to secure the missing rear stowage boxes. The central upper bracket for the jack can still be seen. This feature replaced the straps bolted to the rear of the hull on the early version of the Panther Ausf. G hull. (© *U.S. Army Armor and Cavalry Collection*)

This is the horseshoe-shaped central upper bracket for the 20-tonne jack. The small square blocks welded to the rear armoured plate with the hole in the middle were introduced to secure sheet metal covers around the exhaust pipes to hide their red glow when they were very hot. (© *U.S. Army Armor and Cavalry Collection*)

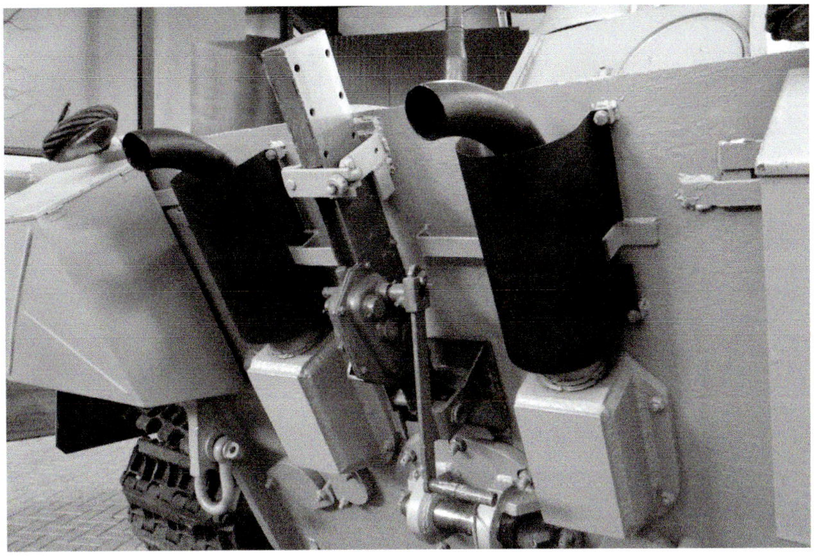

In this photograph of a restored Panzer V Ausf. G, you can see the Panther tank's 20-tonne jack strapped to the rear of the tank, the stowage boxes, and the sheet metal covers around the exhaust pipes.

The original curved cast armoured exhaust guard that was fitted to the early production Panther Ausf. G hulls was replaced with this type of rectangular welded armoured exhaust guard. On later models, this was again replaced by a different style of curved cast armoured exhaust guard. (© *U.S. Army Armor and Cavalry Collection*)

The large circular hatch between the two rectangular welded armoured exhaust guards is the engine access hatch. A large tow bracket is welded to its face. Below that bracket is the armoured cover for the starter. Above the engine access hatch is the lower bracket for the 20-tonne jack. The open armoured cover on the far right protects the port for the right-side *Kettenspanner* (track tensioner mechanism). (© *U.S. Army Armor and Cavalry Collection*)

The armoured cover on the left protects the port for left track tensioner mechanism. The smaller cover to the right of it protects the *Kühlwasser Heizerät* (cold water heating port). To help start the engine in extremely cold weather, a *Fuchsgerät* (blowtorch) would be inserted into the port. This would heat up the engine coolant. (© *U.S. Army Armor and Cavalry Collection*)

The track drive sprocket wheel is at the front. The rim is reinforced with thirty-two countersunk bolts with crowned nuts held by cotter pins. It also has a 315-mm-diameter armoured hub cap. The rubber-rimmed road-wheels are the replacement production series road-wheels with twenty-four rim bolts instead of the earlier sixteen rim bolt version. (© *U.S. Army Armor and Cavalry Collection*)

At the rear of the tank track is the strengthened idler wheel with 15-mm-wide spokes. (© *U.S. Army Armor and Cavalry Collection*)

The track had six 15-mm-high *Gleitschutzpickein* (chevrons) cast into the track face. The Panther tank's tracks were called 'Kgs 64/660/150'. (© *U.S. Army Armor and Cavalry Collection*)

The end of the track pin nearest the tank hull just had a flat head like a nail. (© *U.S. Army Armor and Cavalry Collection*)

The track pin was secured with a 40-mm retaining ring held in place by a split pin. (© *U.S. Army Armor and Cavalry Collection*)

If the track pin retaining ring broke or became loose, the track pin would be pushed back into position each time it hit the track pin return plate bump welded to the hull wall under the pannier in front of the idler wheel. (© *U.S. Army Armor and Cavalry Collection*)

Above left: A lot of parts are missing from the rear engine deck. Some have been removed awaiting restoration. The two circular covers are the armoured caps for the engine air-intake holes. (© *U.S. Army Armor and Cavalry Collection*)

Above right: The left-side cooling air-exhaust fan drive is damaged. This is an eight-bladed fan. Earlier versions had sixteen blades. Above and below it are the rectangular cooling air-intake ports. (© *U.S. Army Armor and Cavalry Collection*)

This is the underneath view of the Panther Ausf. G tank's cooling air exhaust fan drive armoured cowling guard on the workshop floor. The mesh grill is still in place but has some damage. (© *U.S. Army Armor and Cavalry Collection*)

These are the sliding shutters with a mesh screen that go over the right-side air-intake louvres on the rear engine deck. (© *U.S. Army Armor and Cavalry Collection*)

Bottom view of the Panther Ausf. G tank's *Sandkästen* (engine air filters). They sat on top of the engine. (© *U.S. Army Armor and Cavalry Collection*)

Top view of the Panther Ausf. G tank's *Sandkästen*. They sat on top of the engine. (© *U.S. Army Armor and Cavalry Collection*)

Left: This is the side-armoured *Kampfraumheizung* (combat room heater fan drive) that fitted on top of the engine deck. (© *U.S. Army Armor and Cavalry Collection*)

Below: This is the left side raised armoured engine cooling system fan drive that fitted on top of the Panther Ausf. G's engine deck. It was part of the *Warmluftbeheizung* (a crew compartment warm air heating system). Two slits were cut in the armour plate over the engine compartment, and ducting led towards an opening in the firewall that could be opened to allow warm air into the crew compartment.

To funnel warm air into this duct, six pie-shaped elements, stored next to the fan opening, could be placed over the air exhaust. This would force air, warmed by the engine, into the ducting and towards the crew compartment. To improve the warming of the air, on the right side, the air-intake grills could be closed. Also, to regulate the temperature of the air, crews could leave one or more of the pie-shaped elements closed. An often-used alternative designation is *Kampfraumheizung*. (*Martin Webster/Herbert Ackermans*)

This is an air-intake vent. The Panther has four of them in the engine deck. It is on its side in the picture. A rectangular armoured louvred cover would fit over the opening, and that would be covered by a mesh screen. (*©U.S. Army Armor and Cavalry Collection*)

The redesigned Panther tank gun mantlet with the 'chin guard' was not fitted to all Panther Ausf. G tanks. The 'chin' was intended to stop armour-piercing shells from ricocheting down into the crew compartments. It had a bump stop at the bottom, welded onto the front of the turret. Interlocking rectangular joints were used to help strengthen weld joint of the turret's front armour to the side armour plates. (© *U.S. Army Armor and Cavalry Collection*)

The gun mantlet was fitted with a monocular gunsight aperture with rain guard. Panther Ausf. D and early Ausf. A turrets were fitted with binocular TZF 12 gunsights. These could be identified by two holes side by side visible to the left side of the main gun in the mantlet. Starting in late November–early December 1943, these were replaced by monocular TZF 12a gunsights as fitted to this tank turret. (© *U.S. Army Armor and Cavalry Collection*)

The rear turret crew hatch could be locked from the inside. It swung out to the left of the port to give the crew as much room as possible as they loaded stores or got in and out of the turret. Later versions of the turret, like this one had a handle welded to the back of the hatch as well as above. The semi-circular ridge of metal above the opening is a rain guard. (© *U.S. Army Armor and Cavalry Collection*)

The vertical clamp on the right side of this Panther Ausf. G turret was used to hold *Losterkennungstafeln*. Three were fitted to the turret. The large circular cover housed the *Nahverteidigungswaffe* grenade and smoke round discharger and. In the centre of the photograph is a *Pilze* (mushroom-shaped) socket. It is one of three welded to the turret deck. It has its cap still in place to prevent water entry. A 2-tonne *Behelfskrahn* (makeshift crane) could be mounted on the turret in these sockets to assist in engine and gearbox maintenance. There is a small gap in the weld to enable water to drain. (© *U.S. Army Armor and Cavalry Collection*)

Two *Losterkennungstafeln* clamps were fixed on the front of the turret. This one was welded on top of the front turret armour on the left side of this Panther Ausf. G turret between the U-shaped lifting eye and the rain and debris sheet-metal guard that covered the gap between the top of the gun mantlet and the front of the turret. (© *U.S. Army Armor and Cavalry Collection*)

In the top left corner of this photograph, you can see the third *Losterkennungstafel* clamps welded on top of the front turret armour on the right side of this Panther Ausf. G turret between the U-shaped lifting eye and the rain and debris sheet-metal guard that covered the gap between the top of the gun mantlet and the front of the turret. The large circular feature behind it is the forged armoured cap for the turret's *Rohrausblasevorrichtung* (fume extractor). It has a semi-circular bullet splash guard welded to the turret deck in front of it. Behind that is the armoured cover for the loader's periscope. The rectangular block with three drilled holes was the mount for the *Orterkompass* (compass). (© *U.S. Army Armor and Cavalry Collection*)

The commander's cupola was of the cast dome type with seven periscopes. It was fitted with a metal ring above the periscopes so that an anti-aircraft machine gun mount could be fitted. The *Fliegerbeschussgerät* (7.92-mm MG 34 machine gun mount) fixed on top of the ring. (© *U.S. Army Armor and Cavalry Collection*)

On the forward-facing section of the cupola, a gun sighting vane was welded to the cupola's curved side on a T-shaped bracket. The sighting vane is a gun laying tool that consisted of two triangles. The rear one had a 'V' cut into the top. When the tip of the front triangle was between the rear 'V,' the commander could see where the tank's gun was pointing and whether it was facing the right target. (© *U.S. Army Armor and Cavalry Collection*)

Side view of the commander's gun sighting vane. Between the two periscope armoured covers, you can see one of the cupola's three rain gully slits. They were designed to drain the rainwater that would build up where the cupola hatch would meet the edges of the cupola wall. (© *U.S. Army Armor and Cavalry Collection*)

Aperture in the gun mantlet for the coaxial 7.92-mm MG 34 machine gun. (© *U.S. Army Armor and Cavalry Collection*)

Rear and left-side view of the Panzer V Ausf. G turret with cut-away sections. The welded mortice and tenon joint can be seen at the back of the side turret armour. This is where a section of the rear armour plate fitted into the rectangular hole in the side of the turret armour to help make the joint stronger. (© *U.S. Army Armor and Cavalry Collection*)

The right side of the turret side armour also had the same welded mortice and tenon joint. (© *U.S. Army Armor and Cavalry Collection*)

Top view of the commander's cupola. Six of the seven periscope armoured covers are visible. The seventh is under the cupola hatch. The three rain drainage slits can be seen as well as the rectangular fixing plates for the anti-aircraft machine gun mount ring. (© *U.S. Army Armor and Cavalry Collection*)

This is the gunner's position by the side of the 75-mm KwK 42 L/70 main gun. (© *U.S. Army Armor and Cavalry Collection*)

This is the tank driver's position. Many of the driver's instruments are missing like the circular dials of the tachometer and odometer. The gearbox and gear selector handle can be seen under the rectangular electrical panel that contains fuses, warning gauges, and the starter button. The mount for the driver's swivelling periscope is hanging down from the roof with two left and right handles. (© *U.S. Army Armor and Cavalry Collection*)

This is the loader's position viewed from the rear turret hatch. On the right side of the gun breech block at the back, there is a large hexagonal nut. This is securing the large recoil cylinder to the bracket attached to the gun. The recoil cylinder was designed to hydraulically brake the rearward motion of the gun after firing. It is filled with 9 litres of *Braunark* hydraulic fluid. (© *U.S. Army Armor and Cavalry Collection*)

This is where the commander's seat would be, directly under the cupola which you can see in the roof of the turret. It is missing. The large circular port at the back is the turret rear hatch. To the left of that hatch, hanging down from the turret roof at an angle is the *Nahverteidigungswaffe* (grenade and smoke round discharger). (© *U.S. Army Armor and Cavalry Collection*)

4

PANZER V AUSF. G PANTHER TANK AT FORT BENNING

This Panzer V Ausf. G Panther tank is parked in the open-air tank shelter at Fort Benning, Georgia, USA, next to the AACC's Panther Ausf. A on its right and the Panther II hull on its left. It normally has a tarpaulin over it. (© *U.S. Army Armor and Cavalry Collection*)

In April 1945, this Panzer V Ausf. G Panther tank Fgst.Nr. 121455 was assembled at Grafenwöhr, not at the main MAN plant. The Panther was surrendered to US troops outside Salzburg in Austria. It was photographed with three other Panther tanks, even photographed being inspected by General Patton. For some reason not yet discovered, it was moved to Munich and placed in front of the bomb-damaged Imperial Cinema in Karlsplatz. This tank is often referred to as the 'Munich' Panther tank.

In the early 1970s, it was at the Boatwright tank overhaul facility at Fort Knox. Its working engine was removed and placed inside the Panther II hull. This allowed the Panther II to be driven around the arena at the Patton Museum during special events.

This tank has most of the standard features associated with a late production Panther Ausf. G. This includes the metal loops welded to the side of the turret to enable wire or rope to be run between the loops. This enabled cut branches, reeds, straw, or bushes to be secured to the tank turret side to help camouflage it. These started to be fitted on Panther tanks built from January 1945 onwards. Five were fitted to each side of the turret. The turret was not fitted with the 'chin' mantlet. It did not have the studs on the rear right of the turret for mounting an armoured box to house infrared equipment.

On 24 January 1945, the MAN factory was ordered to stop welding the anti-aircraft gun mount's circular ring on top of the commander's cupola. Instructions were later issued that a simplified device, a metal post, was to be welded onto a cupola periscope guard; this was to serve as a base for a new swivelling anti-aircraft gun mount. These started to be fitted in March 1945. One of these metal posts was fitted to this Panther tank's turret cupola. It still had rubber-tyre return rollers. Most of the road-wheels are rubber-rimmed except for the one on the eighth station at the back of the tank, where an 800-mm steel tyre road-wheel has been fitted.

The track is missing. The last Patton Museum curator, Charles R. Lemon, stated that only a short section was delivered with the tank when it arrived at the Patton Museum from Aberdeen Proving Ground in January 1971. He said, 'according to the curator at the time that section of track was accidentally scrapped during the move to the new museum'.

Panzer V Ausf. G Panther tank Fgst.Nr. 121455 on display outside the bomb-damaged Imperial Cinema in Karlsplatz, Munich. The rear road-wheel is different to the rest. It is an 800-mm steel tyre. (*Herbert Ackermans*)

Panzer V Ausf. G Panther tank Fgst.Nr. 121455 on display at the Patton Museum shortly after it arrived in January 1971 from the Aberdeen Proving Ground. It still has its original camouflage. Only a short section of the track was delivered with the tank. The delivery location stencil markings with the date '21/1/71' on the front of the glacis plate are nearly worn off. (*Patton Museum/ Charles R. Lemons*)

Front view of Panzer V Ausf. G Panther Fgst. Nr. 121455, the 'Munich' Panther. (© *U.S. Army Armor and Cavalry Collection*)

Rear right three-quarter view of the Panther Ausf. G tank. The rear stowage boxes, *Schürzen*, and tracks are missing. (© *U.S. Army Armor and Cavalry Collection*)

Front right three-quarter view of the Panther Ausf. G tank. The straight line of the side, upper armour can clearly be seen. There is no triangular piece of armour at the rear of the tank as on the Panther Ausf. D and Ausf. A hulls. (© *U.S. Army Armor and Cavalry Collection*)

The turret was not fitted with a 'chin' mantlet. The interlocking straight edge mortice armour welds made the joint stronger. The loops used to run wire or rope to secure camouflage material can be seen on the side of the turret. (© *U.S. Army Armor and Cavalry Collection*)

Starting in March 1945, a metal post was welded on top of the front left-side-facing cupola periscope armoured guard. This was to serve as a base for a new swivelling anti-aircraft gun mount. On 24 January 1945, the MAN factory was ordered to stop welding the anti-aircraft gun mount circular ring on top of the commander's cupola. In the centre of the photograph is a *Pilze*. It is one of three welded to the turret deck. It has its cap still in place to prevent water entry. A 2-tonne *Behelfskrahn* could be mounted on the turret in these sockets to assist in engine and gearbox maintenance. (© *U.S. Army Armor and Cavalry Collection*)

The bracket with the two bolt holes was for the gun sighting vanes. In front of that was the square hole where the infrared night vision unit's steel band, which indicated elevation, entered the turret. The horseshoe-shaped weld mark was where the raised armoured guard was sighted in front of the cupola to protect the opening. (*© U.S. Army Armor and Cavalry Collection*)

The right side of the gun mantlet has a lifting post at the top. Below it are two brackets welded on to the armour. A rectangular length of metal, on which were the plug sockets for the infrared optics system, was bolted onto these brackets. (*© U.S. Army Armor and Cavalry Collection*)

The left side of the gun mantlet had a post and a circular cap, which looked very similar to the end of a big nail. There was one on the other side. These were used for lifting the gun mantlet off the turret for repairs. The thin rain and debris guard can be seen on the top as well as the clamp for holding the *Losterkennungstafeln*. (*© U.S. Army Armor and Cavalry Collection*)

The V-shaped block of metal welded to the front of the turret on the left side at the bottom is the gun mantlet bottom bump stop. (© *U.S. Army Armor and Cavalry Collection*)

The loops used to run wire or rope to secure camouflage material can be seen on the side of the turret. These started to be fitted on Panther tank turrets built from January 1945 onwards. Five were fitted to each side of the turret. (© *U.S. Army Armor and Cavalry Collection*)

To increase the strength of the weld between the turret side and rear armour, a large mortice and tenon joint was used. On the bottom right side of the rear circular hatch, a bracket with a hole was fitted. This was to enable the hatch to be locked from the outside. (© *U.S. Army Armor and Cavalry Collection*)

The top of the rear turret hatch seal was protected by a rain guard. Starting in June 1944, a handle was welded onto the back of the large circular escape hatch at the rear of the turret. The small circular fitting in the top right of the photograph is a *Pilze*. It is one of three welded to the turret deck. It has its cap still in place to prevent water entry. A 2-tonne *Behelfskrahn* crane could be mounted on the turret in these sockets to assist in suspension, engine, and gearbox maintenance. (© *U.S. Army Armor and Cavalry Collection*)

The rear turret hatch lock was welded onto the armour plate between the two cone-shaped bolts that secured the hatch hinge on the inside of the turret. (© *U.S. Army Armor and Cavalry Collection*)

Starting in September 1944, the gunsight aperture rain guard was lengthened as rainwater was still entering the hole. This monocular gunsight on the left of the gun has the lengthened version. (© *U.S. Army Armor and Cavalry Collection*)

From this angle, the depth of the monocular gunsight rain guard can be better appreciated. (© *U.S. Army Armor and Cavalry Collection*)

This is the coaxial 7.92-mm MG 34 machine gun aperture on the right side of the gun mantlet. (© *U.S. Army Armor and Cavalry Collection*)

The rectangular piece of metal with two holes in it welded to the front right side of the turret is the base plate for the two-part clamp used for holding a *Losterkennungstafeln*. Two others were welded on to the turret in locations that were visible from the commander's cupola when the hatch was locked in the closed position. (© *U.S. Army Armor and Cavalry Collection*)

The second clamp on the front left side of the turret is also for holding a *Losterkennungstafeln*. It is missing its top part and wing nuts. (© *U.S. Army Armor and Cavalry Collection*)

The third clamp is on the rear right side of the turret. It is for holding a *Losterkennungstafeln*. The round plate bolted to the turret roof is covering the hole where the 360-degree *Nahverteidigungswaffe* would have been fixed. (© *U.S. Army Armor and Cavalry Collection*)

This armoured cast dome on the turret roof protects the exhaust fan. The semi-circular guard in front protects the side openings and stops bullets and shrapnel entering the side openings. (© *U.S. Army Armor and Cavalry Collection*)

The front glacis plate and lower hull armour plate were welded to the hull side armour using interlocking rectangular joints to increase the strength of the intersection. (© *U.S. Army Armor and Cavalry Collection*)

The front glacis plate and lower hull armour plate were also welded together using interlocking rectangular joints to increase the strength of the intersection. The hole in the side armour at the front of the Panther tank was used when the tank was lifted or towed. The front mudguard here is a replacement item, not the original one. (© *U.S. Army Armor and Cavalry Collection*)

The Panzer V Ausf. G Panther tank hull was fitted with a 7.92-mm MG 34 machine gun in a cast armoured guard around a ball mount. (© *U.S. Army Armor and Cavalry Collection*)

There is a thick lip around the bottom of the machine gun ball mount. This was to reduce enemy bullet splash entering the mount's aperture, having first hit the sloped glacis plate below the mount and ricocheted upwards. (© *U.S. Army Armor and Cavalry Collection*)

This is the upper right-side rectangular interlocking armour weld joint between the 80-mm-thick glacis plate and the 50-mm superstructure side armour plate. On the top of the hull roof is the armoured guard for the hull machine gunner's periscope. (© *U.S. Army Armor and Cavalry Collection*)

The driver's periscope could swivel to give him better vision. It had an armoured cover. He no longer had a vision hatch in the glacis plate. (© *U.S. Army Armor and Cavalry Collection*)

Right-side rectangular interlocking armour weld joints between the 80-mm-thick glacis plate and the 55-mm lower hull armour plate. (© *U.S. Army Armor and Cavalry Collection*)

The central rectangular interlocking armour weld joint between the 80-mm-thick glacis plate and the 50-mm lower hull armour plate. (© *U.S. Army Armor and Cavalry Collection*)

Left-side rectangular interlocking armour weld joints between the 80-mm-thick glacis plate and the 55-mm lower hull armour plate. (© *U.S. Army Armor and Cavalry Collection*)

On the right of the vehicle is the hull machine gunner's periscope armoured guard. In the middle is the gun travel lock over the hull cabin vent armoured cover. (© *U.S. Army Armor and Cavalry Collection*)

Just under the gun barrel is the driver's swivelling periscope and armoured cover. The gun travel lock would normally be fixed over the hull cabin vent armoured cover, but it is missing. (© *U.S. Army Armor and Cavalry Collection*)

The driver's and hull machine gunner's hatches are missing. The armoured hull decking into which those hatches would have been attached is also missing. It has a temporary metal cover. (© *U.S. Army Armor and Cavalry Collection*)

The big stowage bins are missing from the rear of the tank. (© *U.S. Army Armor and Cavalry Collection*)

The large circular hatch between the two curved cast armoured exhaust guards is the engine access hatch. A large tow bracket is welded to its face. Below that bracket is the armoured cover for the starter. (© *U.S. Army Armor and Cavalry Collection*)

The armoured cover on the left protects the port for the *Kettenspanner* (left track tensioner mechanism). The smaller cover to the right of it protects the *Kühlwasser Heizerät*. To help start the engine in extremely cold weather, a blowtorch would be inserted into the port. This would heat up the engine coolant. (© *U.S. Army Armor and Cavalry Collection*)

The armoured cover on the far right protects the port for the *Kettenspanner* (right track tensioner mechanism). (© *U.S. Army Armor and Cavalry Collection*)

The exit point of the engine's exhaust pipe through the rear armour caused a weak spot in the armour. It was protected by a curved cast armoured cover. On middle production models, these were changed for a welded box-like armoured exhaust cover. (© *U.S. Army Armor and Cavalry Collection*)

The exhaust pipes got very hot and glowed red. At night, this could give away the tank's location. Sheet metal shields were later introduced to hide the red glow. These would then be replaced by a tubular *Flammenvernichter* (heat guard) that fitted over the pipes. (© *U.S. Army Armor and Cavalry Collection*)

Above left: To the left of the armoured exhaust cover and above the engine access disc is a rectangular indent. This was where the bottom bracket for the 20-tonne jack would have been fitted. (© *U.S. Army Armor and Cavalry Collection*)

Above right: To try and reduce flames coming out of the top of the exhaust pipes and debris getting in them, caps were fitted to the top. Only the right-side exhaust pipe still has its cap fitted. (© *U.S. Army Armor and Cavalry Collection*)

A mudguard was fitted over the top of the track as it went around the rear idler wheel. (© *U.S. Army Armor and Cavalry Collection*)

This is the underneath of the mudguard that was fitted over the top of the track as it went around the rear idler wheel. (© *U.S. Army Armor and Cavalry Collection*)

Both rear mudguards are still present on this tank. (© *U.S. Army Armor and Cavalry Collection*)

The earlier Panther II hull had a hole drilled into the top of the rear, side hull armour. The Panther Ausf. G had a hook. Both these features were used to attach chains to enable the tank to be lifted for transportation or mechanical repair. (© *U.S. Army Armor and Cavalry Collection*)

A hole was drilled into the bottom of the rear, side hull armour. This was used to attach towing cables. (© *U.S. Army Armor and Cavalry Collection*)

Rear right-side rectangular engine cooling air-intake vents on the engine deck. It is missing its mesh cover. (© *U.S. Army Armor and Cavalry Collection*)

Rear right-side circular armoured guard and mesh cover over the engine air exhaust fan next to one of the two circular armoured caps for the engine air-intake holes. The later versions had handles on them. (© *U.S. Army Armor and Cavalry Collection*)

Forward right-side rectangular engine cooling air-intake vent armoured guard on the engine deck. It is missing its mesh cover. (© *U.S. Army Armor and Cavalry Collection*)

The two circular armoured caps are for the engine air-intake holes. The square vent behind them is the armoured deflector for the air-intake. A hose or snorkel could be attached to this intake when the tank was undertaking deep river fording. (© *U.S. Army Armor and Cavalry Collection*)

The rear left-side rectangular engine cooling air-intake vents on the engine deck has its armoured guard and mesh cover fitted with sliding shutters. These would be closed when the tank was fording a deep river. (© *U.S. Army Armor and Cavalry Collection*)

This is the *Warmluftbeheizung*. (© *U.S. Army Armor and Cavalry Collection*)

Forward left-side, rectangular engine cooling air-intake vent armoured guard and mesh cover on the engine deck. It does not have a sliding shutter fitted. (© *U.S. Army Armor and Cavalry Collection*)

Left-side view of the *Warmluftbeheizung*. (© *U.S. Army Armor and Cavalry Collection*)

Right-side view of the *Warmluftbeheizung*. You can also see the angled back of the armoured deflector for the middle air-intake vent. (© *U.S. Army Armor and Cavalry Collection*)

The vertical side hull armour was 40 mm thick. (© *U.S. Army Armor and Cavalry Collection*)

The *Schürzen* bracket rail still runs the whole length of the right side of the tank. (© *U.S. Army Armor and Cavalry Collection*)

The *Schürzen* bracket rail has been damaged and only runs along the rear section of the left side of the tank. (© *U.S. Army Armor and Cavalry Collection*)

The *Schürzen* bracket was attached to the debris guard metal sheet by a nut and bolt. (© *U.S. Army Armor and Cavalry Collection*)

The debris guard metal sheet was attached to the *Schürzen* bracket by a nut and bolt. (© *U.S. Army Armor and Cavalry Collection*)

An L-shaped bracket was welded to the side of the side superstructure armour plate, along with two nuts and bolts, was used to join two sections of the *Schürzen* debris guard metal sheet. (© *U.S. Army Armor and Cavalry Collection*)

To support the *Schürzen* debris guard metal sheet along its length, an L-shaped bracket was welded to the side superstructure armour plate, and a nut and bolt used. (© *U.S. Army Armor and Cavalry Collection*)

This is another style of *Schürzen* panel debris guard metal sheet support bracket. (© *U.S. Army Armor and Cavalry Collection*)

The track drive sprocket wheel is at the front. The rim is reinforced with thirty-two countersunk bolts with crowned nuts held by cotter pins. It also has a 315-mm-diameter armoured hub cap. (© *U.S. Army Armor and Cavalry Collection*)

The rubber-rimmed road-wheels were designed to be interleaved. This helped spread the weight of the Panther tank over the wide track. The interleaved layout also provided the Panther and Tigers with much better floatation, compared to even the much lighter Shermans, which had larger gaps between their respective road-wheels. (© *U.S. Army Armor and Cavalry Collection*)

The rubber-rimmed road-wheels are the replacement production series road-wheels with twenty-four rim bolts instead of the earlier sixteen rim bolt version. (© *U.S. Army Armor and Cavalry Collection*)

This later version rear 665-mm-diameter idler wheel was designed for improved self-cleaning. (© *U.S. Army Armor and Cavalry Collection*)

If the rear road-wheel was damaged and needed changing, four wheels had to be removed. (© *U.S. Army Armor and Cavalry Collection*)

The curved box-like structure above the first road-wheel behind the sprocket wheel is the *Anschlagblock* (suspension swing arm bump stop). (© *U.S. Army Armor and Cavalry Collection*)

The bolted fixture on the hull wall with the two springs is another type of *Anschlagblock*. (© *U.S. Army Armor and Cavalry Collection*)

The armoured belly plate at the front of the Panther Ausf. G was 25 mm thick. (© *U.S. Army Armor and Cavalry Collection*)

The armoured belly plates in the middle and the rear were 16 mm thick. Access ports and drain holes were built into the belly plates. (© *U.S. Army Armor and Cavalry Collection*)

5

PANZER V AUSF. A PANTHER TANK AT THE AMERICAN HERITAGE MUSEUM

Panther tank 501 can be found in the '1944 Clash of Steel' section of the American Heritage Museum. (*© AHM*)

The new American Heritage Museum opened its doors to the public in May 2019. Owen Myers from the American Heritage Museum has researched the history of their Panzer V Ausf. A (No. 501) Panther tank. He stated that it was issued to the 2nd Panzer Regiment of the 16th Panzer Division in July 1944; this was probably while the division was stationed in Daleszyce, Poland, taking part in anti-partisan operations. The town was a *de facto* centre for the Polish Resistance and was eventually destroyed in late 1944. The 16th Panzer Division then took part in an attempt to repel the Soviet Vistula–Oder offensive.

They fought near the town of Bieleckie Młyny but were under constant bombardment from tanks, artillery fire, and fighter-bombers. The crew tried to cross the Nida river, which in most places is only 3–4 feet deep. Unfortunately, the spot in the river they attempted to cross was around 6 feet deep. The Nida is one of Poland's warmest rivers. Even in the middle of a very cold Polish winter, the ice is relatively thin. This Panther broke through the ice and was stuck in the water up to turret level. To keep the tank from being captured, the crew placed explosives in the turret and 'scuttled' it before retreating on foot to German lines further to the west. The 16th Panzer Division eventually surrendered to Soviet and American forces in Czechoslovakia in May 1945.

While other tanks were recovered and scrapped, this Panther was left in the Nida river for around fifty years because of the difficulty of pulling it out of the water. The constant flow of freshwater kept the hull in relatively decent shape, preserving much of it, but what was left of the turret was exposed to the elements and had severely rotted. Only the mantlet and a few parts of the gun and breech were recovered and could be restored. The tank was recovered in November 1990 by a German collector, who sold it back to the Polish state. It was eventually sold as a hulk to Jacques Littlefield in around 2000, who began restoration in 2003–2004. It was featured in episode two of the TV documentary *Tank Overhaul* while it was still being restored. This is often repeated on television and can be seen on YouTube. It was finally finished the same year of Jacques Littlefield's untimely death on 7 January 2009.

When the collection was sold off by the Littlefield estate, it was purchased by the Collings Foundation to be one of the stars of their new land warfare museum. It is now displayed in the centre of the '1944 Clash of Steel' section of the Second World War hangar opposite a Soviet T-34-85 medium tank—its main enemy on the Eastern Front. Visitors can walk around the Panther and view it from every angle, including from above as there is a viewing platform to its right side and in front of it. The quality of the restoration is of the highest standard, both internally and outside. Care has been taken to find tools, spare track links, and equipment to fix to the outer hull.

The American Heritage Museum is located at 568 Main Street, Hudson, Massachusetts. It is 27 miles (43.45 km) west of Boston and takes about one hour to get there by car. The Collings Foundation is a non-profit, educational foundation. The stated purpose of the foundation is to organise and support 'living history' events that enable Americans to learn more about their heritage through direct participation. International visitors can learn a lot, as well. Check their website for opening hours.

The restoration of the American Heritage Museum's Panther Ausf. A is of the highest quality. (*© AHM*)

The German Panther Ausf. A tank is displayed opposite a Soviet T-34-85 in the '1944 Clash of Steel' section of the American Heritage Museum. (*© AHM*)

On the Panzer V Ausf. A, the gap between the top of the wheels and the panniers was covered by plates of *Schürzen* (side skirt armour) suspended on hangers. They were designed to stop Soviet anti-tank rifle rounds. You can also see in this photograph that the tank has been fitted with the newer replacement production series road-wheels with twenty-four rim bolts rather than the earlier sixteen rim bolt version. (*© AHM*)

The rear armour on the Panther Ausf. A was 40 mm thick and angled at 30 degrees. The side superstructure armour covering the internal stowage panniers was 40 mm thick and angled at 40 degrees. The side hull armour was also 40 mm thick but vertical. (*© AHM*)

The two holes in the gun mantlet indicate that this Panther was fitted with a binocular TZF 12 gunsight. Starting in late November–early December 1943, these were replaced by monocular TZF 12a gunsights. The binocular sight has a semi-circular rain guard over it. (*© AHM*)

The circular hole in the gun mantlet, on the right of the gun, is the aperture for the coaxial 7.92-mm MG 34 machine gun. (*© AHM*)

The dome-shaped commander's cupola was introduced after production had started on the Ausf. A version of the Panther tank turret. Not all of them had this type of cupola at first. The cast armour dome-shaped cupola body was inset with seven periscopes that were protected by armoured cowlings. (*© AHM*)

Starting from 1 August 1943, factories were instructed to fit an anti-aircraft machine gun mounting ring to the top of the commander's cupola. Brackets were welded onto the top of the armoured periscope housing. (*© AHM*)

The *Fliegerbeschussgerät* (7.92-mm MG 34 machine gun mount) was fixed on top of the anti-aircraft machine gun mounting ring to the top of the commander's cupola. (*© AHM*)

The front of the commander's cupola had a sighting vane, a gun laying tool, that consisted of two triangles. The rear one had a 'V' cut into the top. When the tip of the front triangle was between the rear 'V', the commander could see where the tank's gun was pointing and whether it was facing the right target. (*© AHM*)

Ammunition for the 7.92-mm MG 34 machine gun was kept in a canvas bag to the left side of the gun. (*© AHM*)

Under the machine gun is a vertical metal post. It is a bump stop for the cupola hatch; when it swung back when being closed, the hatch hits the stop and drops into the recess. (*© AHM*)

When the hatch is opened, it raises up to clear the top of the cupola. (*© AHM*)

Many cupola hatches on other tanks flip upwards. This increases their height and makes them easier to target. The Panther tank's cupola hatch raises and then rotates sideways. (*© AHM*)

The 1 o'clock to 12 o'clock azimuth indicator ring fitted inside the commander's cupola. (*© AHM*)

This is the armoured cover for the turret deck's *Rohrausblasevorrichtung*. The vents that face forward and to the side are protected by a semi-circular welded armoured guard. (*© AHM*)

The oval disk on the right with the four screws is the cover for the *Nahverteidgungswaffe*. The loader's periscope is in front of that, just to the rear of the circular armoured cover over the *Rohrausblasevorrichtung*. (*© AHM*)

This inverted U-shaped lug on top of the turret deck was used for lifting the turret off the hull. (*© AHM*)

The few Panther Ausf. A tanks completed after May 1944 had handles fitted to the rear turret escape hatches in the factory. The earlier Ausf. A turrets were not fitted with this handle. Most handles fitted to Ausf. A turrets were done as later field modifications. (*© AHM*)

The large circular hatch at the back of the turret made it easy to load ammunition and supplies. If the tank was hit, turret crew had an easy escape route. (*© AHM*)

Rear right-side rectangular engine cooling air-intake vent on the engine deck next to the circular armoured guard and mesh cover over the engine air-exhaust fan. (© *AHM*)

The two circular armoured caps with handles are for the engine air-intake holes. (© *AHM*)

This is the left side of the rear engine deck. The rectangular armoured grill and mesh protect the air-intake louvres. The large circular armoured grill and mesh protect the hot air-exhaust fan. (© *AHM*)

This Panther Ausf. A only has two exhaust pipes. Two thinner cooling pipes were later fitted to the left exhaust pipe armoured cover on later versions. (*© AHM*)

Not all surviving Panther tanks have rear stowage boxes fitted. (*© AHM*)

The hatch to the rear stowage boxes could be locked with a padlock. In all armies, theft of kit and food was rife during the war. (*© AHM*)

To the right of the left-side stowage box is the curved rectangular top cover of the rear convoy light. (*© AHM*)

The hole where the exhaust pipe protruded out of the rear armour plate was a weak spot that could be targeted by the enemy. The designers surrounded it in a curved cast armoured guard. Over the production period, the Panther tank had many different types of exhaust guards. (*© AHM*)

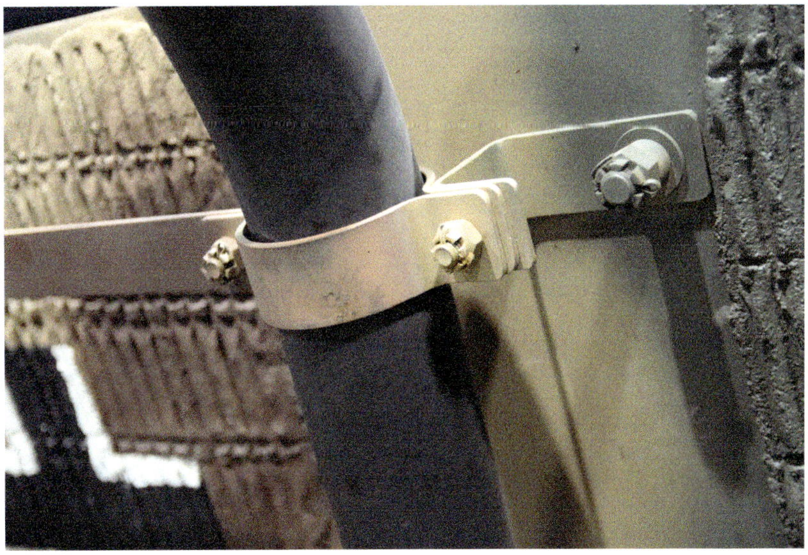

The nuts that held the metal exhaust pipe securing straps in place were stopped from coming loose by the use of a split pin. (*© AHM*)

The grey heavy lifting jack was secured to the back of the tank in front of the circular engine access hatch. (© *AHM*)

The early Panzer Ausf. A tanks still had an armoured vision hatch for the driver. In later versions of the Panther, it was removed and replaced by a swivelling periscope in the hull roof. This simplified production and removed a weak spot in the front glacis armour plate. (© *AHM*)

The Panther Ausf. D and early production Panther Ausf. A hulls still had the 'letterbox' machine gun opening in the glacis plate. Starting late November–early December 1943, it was replaced by a ball mount for the hull 7.92-mm MG 34 machine gun. (© *AHM*)

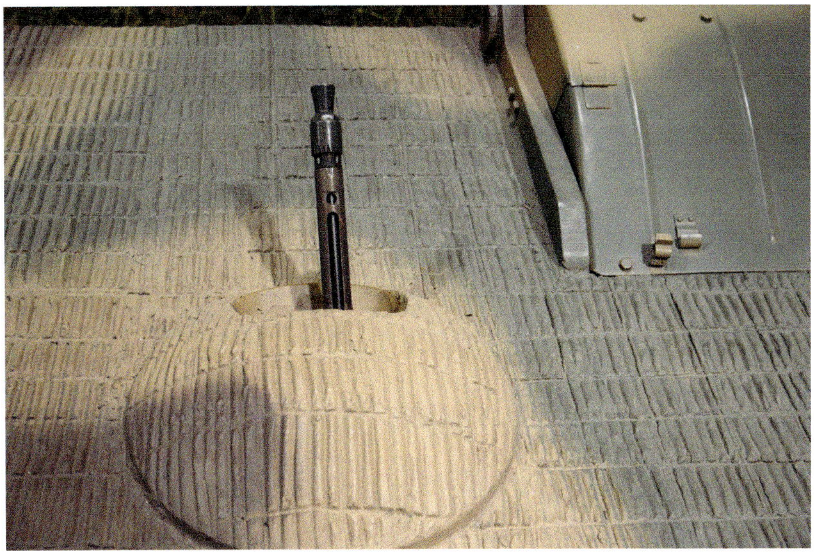

Zimmerit was also applied to the armoured cover for the 7.92-mm MG 34 machine gun ball mount. (*© AHM*)

The tank's main gun was locked into position when it was being driven outside a combat area to protect it from damage and wear. When the clamp was not being used, it rested on top of the hull deck. (*© AHM*)

The driver's vision hatch was raised when not in a combat area to improve the field of view and help with ventilation. (*© AHM*)

The early production Panther Ausf. D hulls had two Bosch *Tarnlampe* bolted to the front glacis plate, one on each side. Starting from September 1943, only one headlight, with a blackout cover, was fitted to the left side of the tank. The Ausf. A tank hulls also only had one headlight bolted to the glacis plate on the left side. (*© AHM*)

The C-shaped hook attached to the side of the Panther was used to connect the oval eye of the towing cable to the towing brackets or eyes on the tank. (*© AHM*)

Large chained split pins kept it from falling off the two tubular posts. (*© AHM*)

The oval-shaped eye of the towing cable can be seen above the wire cutters and fire extinguisher. (*© AHM*)

This block of wood is often attached to the outside of German tanks and self-propelled guns. It is the hard base for the jack. (*© AHM*)

A large chained split pin is used to keep the oval eye of the towing cable from falling off when the tank is moving. (*© AHM*)

The tube attached to the side of the Panther tank is a cylindrical stowage bin for the main gun cleaning rods and brush. The spare radio antenna rods were also kept inside. (© *AHM*)

Hanger brackets were used to attach the protective *Schürzen* around the side of the Panther. They were designed to defeat the Soviet 14.5-mm anti-tank rifle round and give added protection to the vertical 40-mm hull side armour. (© *AHM*)

The caps for the cylindrical stowage bin was held in place by clips and a chain retainer. (© *AHM*)

Spare tank tracks could be strapped to the side of the tank hull at the rear. (© *AHM*)

The post at the end of the hull was used to secure the tow cable. The two brackets are for attaching spare tank tracks. (© *AHM*)

The wide tank tracks helped reduce ground pressure. There were eighty-seven track links per side. They were called Kgs 64/660/150. Chevrons were part of the track design to help give extra grip. (© *AHM*)

The final drive was at the front of the tank and powered sprocket wheels, which had seventeen teeth that locked into the holes on the track. (*© AHM*)

Starting in August 1943, reinforced inner and outer road-wheels with twenty-four rim bolts were introduced. The earlier version of tank road-wheels used on the Panther Ausf. D only had sixteen rim bolts. (*© AHM*)

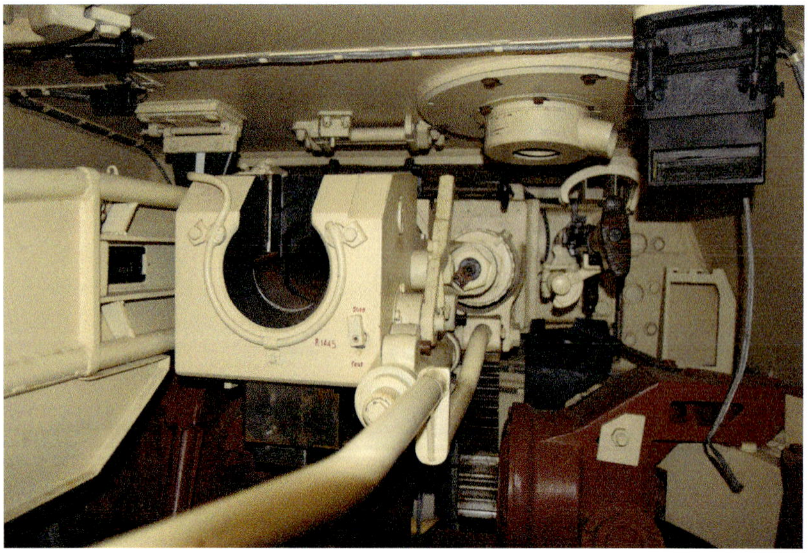

The 7.5-cm KwK 42 L/70 gun breech and coaxial 7.92-mm MG 34 machine gun. (*© AHM*)

Most Panther Ausf. G tanks were fitted with a FuG 5 radio set and an internal intercom. Platoon leaders and company HQ tanks were fitted with an additional FuG 2 radio to communicate on the command channel.

The hull 7.92-mm MG 34 machine gun and radio operator's position. (*© AHM*)

Rear view of the 7.92-mm MG 34 machine gun ball mounting and armoured cover. The gunsight has a green protective eye cushion around it. (*© AHM*)

This is the driver's seat. There is a black and silver diagram to the right that shows the gear stick selector positions. (*© AHM*)

In front of the driver are the final drive and the track brake levers. (*© AHM*)

This is the view from the cupola looking down into the turret. The lower seat is for the turret gunner, and the larger nearer one is for the tank commander. (*© AHM*)

This is the view looking backwards into the fighting compartment. The long grey rectangular box on the floor has two flaps in it. This is where the used tank gun shells go. (*© AHM*)

The black sided stowage box with holes in the top was used to hold ammunition for the main gun. (*© AHM*)

The new turret design used on the Panzer V Ausf. A was simplified. Early production Ausf. A turrets still had the pistol ports in the turret. On turrets built after June 1944, like this one, there are no longer small circular pistol ports in the sides and rear of the turret. The additional circular communication hatch used for loading shells and throwing out used shell casings was no longer cut into the turret side armour. You can also see the new domed cast armour commander's cupola; early versions had a straight-sided drum-shaped cupola. (*© AHM*)

APPENDIX

SURVIVING PANTHER TANKS

Always phone the museum or local town hall to see if the tank is still there before driving to the location as tanks move. That may seem a silly statement, but tanks often change locations. Some are sold, shipped out to take part in military vehicle events, or temporarily transferred to other museums. Others are withdrawn from public view to enable them to be restored or undergo maintenance. Some tanks are on military bases (e.g. Thun in Switzerland and WTS Trier in Germany) and may not be open to the public. A number of the tanks in this list are in private collections and are not open to the general public.

PANTHER AUSF. D (NO. 534), BREDA, HOLLAND (THE NETHERLANDS)

This is the only surviving Panther Ausf. D. It can be seen at the road junction of *Wilhelminapark* and *Paule Windhausenweg* in Breda, Holland (The Netherlands). It was donated by troops of the Polish 1st Armoured Division to serve as a memorial to their fallen comrades and their part in the liberation of Breda in 1944. It was restored in 2004–2005 for static display by Kevin Wheatcroft in exchange for the engine and gearbox to be used on a working Panther restoration.

Panzer V Ausf. D Panther tank (No. 534) in Breda.

PANTHER AUSF. D, THE HOEBIG PRIVATE COLLECTION, GERMANY

A second surviving Panther Ausf. D tank is believed to be part of the Hoebig Private Collection. This information has not been verified. No photographs have been published.

PANTHER II TANK AT FORT BENNING, GEORGIA, USA

See Chapter 1.

PANZER V AUSF. A PANTHER TANK AT FORT BENNING, GEORGIA, USA

See Chapter 2.

PANZER V AUSF. A PANTHER TANK AT THE AMERICAN HERITAGE MUSEUM, MA, USA

See Chapter 5.

PANTHER AUSF. A, PANZERMUSEUM, THUN, SWITZERLAND

This Panther Ausf. A tank can be seen at the *Panzermuseum*, Thun, Switzerland. Its hull number is 210530. It was assembled in December 1943 but still has the 16-mm belly plate. This is a mid-production Ausf. A hull with a mid-production or late Ausf. A turret. The mantlet is a replica.

Left: Rear view of the Panzer V Ausf. A Panther tank at the *Panzermuseum* in Thun. (*Massimo Foti*)

Right: Panzer V Ausf. A Panther tank at the *Panzermuseum* in Thun. (*Massimo Foti*)

PANTHER AUSF. A, THE WHEATCROFT COLLECTION, ENGLAND (THREE VEHICLES)

The Wheatcroft collection is based in Leicestershire, England. They have three Panzer V Ausf. A Panther tanks currently undergoing restoration and a fourth Panther tank that is believed to be an Ausf. G but this has not been confirmed.

The tank shown in the photographs below is an early production Ausf. A. Its hull and turret number is *Fahrgestell Nummer* 158134. The type of *Zimmerit* pattern used on the tank and some of the fittings suggests that it was built at the Demag factory at Falkensee and rolled off the production line in November 1943. The front glacis plate still has the 'letterbox' opening hatch for the hull machine gunner. The turret is also an early production version as it still has pistol ports in the side and rear of the armour, but it does have the later dome-shaped (not drum-shaped) commander's cupola, and there is a handle fitted onto the circular rear crew hatch. Two photographs dated 9 March 1945 have been found of the tank in Le Val du Breuil, 2 miles north-west of Briouze, Normandy. A third photograph showed that it was moved from that location nearer the road and some houses. It had two different unit numbers on the turret. The number 103 was later overpainted by a larger number 231. This tank had been used as a 'hard target' on a French Army firing range.

A second Panzer V Ausf. A Panther tank undergoing restoration is a later production Ausf. A version. The front glacis plate has a *Kugelblende* (machine gun ball mount) fitted instead of the 'letterbox' opening hatch for the hull machine gunner. It suffered severe damage on the upper glacis plate from a direct hit by a shell while being used as a 'hard target' on a French Army firing range.

The third Panzer V Ausf. A Panther tank is also a later production Ausf. A version. The front glacis plate has a *Kugelblende* fitted instead of the 'letterbox' opening hatch for the hull machine gunner. The turret still has pistol ports in the side and rear armour. It is awaiting restoration.

Left: Panzer V Ausf. A Panther tank turret at The Wheatcroft Collection. (*Mark Barnes*)

Right: Panzer V Ausf. A Panther tank hull at The Wheatcroft Collection. Photographed using a 'fish-eye' lens to get the whole hull deck in one image. (*Mark Barnes*)

PANTHER AUSF. A *BEFEHLSPANZER*, PANZERMUSEUM, MÜNSTER, GERMANY

A Panther Ausf. A *Befehlspanzer* (Command tank) is at the *Deutsches Panzermuseum*, Münster. It is in running condition. This tank was bought by Sweden in 1948 for trial purposes. It was given back to the *Panzerlehrbrigade* at Münster in 1960. Some years later, it was handed over to the *Panzertruppenschule* (tank crew school). In the 1980s, the commander of the *Panzertruppenschule* initiated a total restoration. Also, the original Maybach HL 230 engine was overhauled by MTU at Friedrichshafen. After some problems with the HL 230 engine and the lack of spare parts, the engine was replaced by a modern MTU Diesel. The sound of this tank, while being moved, is not original (Information from Rudi Ehninger, Brigadier General (rtd.) German *Panzertruppe*).

Panzer V Ausf. A Panther *Befehlspanzer* (Command tank) at the *Deutsches Panzermuseum*. (*Massimo Foti*)

PANTHER AUSF. A (NOS 224 AND 243), AUTO AND TECHNIK MUSEUM, SINSHEIM, GERMANY

This Panther Ausf. A No. 224 is on display at the Auto and Technik Museum in Sinsheim. This tank was originally given by the *Musée des Blindés* (Museum of Armour), Saumur, to the WTS Koblenz. When the WTS received their Panther Ausf. G from the British Army Defence Academy in Shrivenham, this one was handed over to the Auto and Technik Museum, (Information from Rudi Ehninger, Brigadier General (rtd) German *Panzertruppe*).

This Panther Ausf. A No. 243 wreck is also on display at the Auto and Technik Museum, Sinsheim. It was found in a bog near the town of Spola in Ukraine. It still has its original paint and markings.

Left: The Panzer V Ausf. A Panther tank (No. 224) is on display at the Auto and Technik Museum. (*Massimo Foti*)

Right: The Panzer V Ausf. A Panther tank (No. 243) is on display at the Auto and Technik Museum. (*Massimo Foti*)

PANTHER AUSF. A (NO. 413), THE HOEBIG PRIVATE COLLECTION, GERMANY

This Panther Ausf. A (No. 413) is part of the Hoebig Private Collection in Germany. It was part of the 116th Panzer Division '*Windhund*' and was lost near Falaise. It has been restored. The tank consists of 90 per cent original parts, some of which have come from other Panthers.

The Panzer V Ausf. A Panther tank (No. 413) is part of the Hoebig Private Collection in Germany.

PANTHER AUSF. A (NOS 211 AND 256), MUSÉE DES BLINDÉS, SAUMUR, FRANCE

The Panther Ausf. A (No. 211) tank can be seen at the *Musée des Blindés* (Museum of Armour), Saumur, France. The turret comes from another Panther (hull number 152451), which is currently preserved in the Omaha Overlord Museum, Colleville-sur-Mer, France.

The Panther Ausf. A (No. 256) tank can be seen at the *Musée des Blindés*. It left the factory gate on 2 June 1944 and was recovered by AMX. It was obtained from the French *Etablissement d'Expérimentation Technique de Bourges* (ETBS: Tank Proving Ground in Bourges, France) after they had finished conducting tests. It has been restored to a running condition.

The Panzer V Ausf. A Panther tank (No. 211) can be seen at the *Musée des Blindés*. (*Massimo Foti*)

The Panzer V Ausf. A Panther tank (No. 256) can be seen at the *Musée des Blindés*. (*Massimo Foti*)

PANTHER AUSF. A, OMAHA OVERLORD MUSEUM, COLLEVILLE-SUR-MER, FRANCE

This Panther Ausf. A tank can be seen at the Omaha Overlord Museum, Colleville-sur-Mer, France. It is displayed in a mock-up of a German Army field maintenance and repair yard. It was constructed by Daimler-Benz and had the hull number 152451. It was built in April–May 1944. In January 1945, French Army Captain Besnier of 1 GMR went to Ranes, Normandy, looking for abandoned functional German tanks. On 23 January 1945, he returned to Arthon with some German vehicles, including two Panzer IV tanks and this Panther tank, plus an artillery gun. By April 1945, this Panther was restored to running condition and served in the French Army after the Second World War. It was part of the French *6ème Cuirs, 2ème escadron*.

It spent some time during the 1950s in the city of Baumholder, Germany. In 1955, it returned to Satory, France, where it was then transferred to the French ETBS for tests (Lot 44 in the inventory). In 1980, it was moved from Bourges to Saumur on the order of Colonel Aubry. In 1988, it was swapped for a German Sdkfz 251 halftrack belonging to the now-closed Falaise Museum.

The damage on the front was done during a test at the ETBS. The barrel comes from Southern France (Perpignan area); the turret is not original to the hull. The original turret from this hull was used to restore Saumur Panther No. 254. The tank was transferred from Falaise to the new museum in January 2013.

This Panzer V Ausf. A Panther tank can be seen at the Omaha Overlord Museum.

PANTHER AUSF. A, 501/503E MOURMELON-LE-GRAND, FRANCE

This Panther Ausf. A is on display at the French Army barracks of the 501/503e regiment in Mourmelon-le-Grand, France. It has the hull number 155597 and was built in the MNH factory between July and August 1944. It was abandoned in the Jardin du Senat after the Battle of Paris in August 1944. It was then displayed with a Panther Ausf. G in front of the Hôtel National des Invalides, Paris. In 1976, both tanks were transferred to Saumur. The Panther Ausf. G was captured during the Battle of Dompaire in September 1944 and is still preserved in Saumur. The French Army did use Panther tanks from 1945 to 1952, in the 503rd RCC and the 6e *Cuir*.

This Panzer V Ausf. A Panther tank is on display at the French Army barracks of the 501/503e Regiment in Mourmelon-le-Grand. (*Pierre-Olivier Buan*)

PANTHER AUSF. A, ROYAL JORDANIAN TANK MUSEUM, JORDAN

This Panther Ausf. A tank was previously part of the Saumur Tank Museum collection. In 2010, it was part of an exchange of vehicles between the French president and King Abdullah II of Jordan. It is now on display in the Royal Tank Museum, Amman, Jordan. It is not in running condition as it does not have an engine or gearbox.

This Panzer V Ausf. A Panther tank is on display in the Royal Tank Museum. (*Tammam Khasawneh Abu Ahmad—Royal Tank Museum, Jordan*)

PANTHER AUSF. A, AUSTRALIAN ARMOUR AND ARTILLERY MUSEUM, CAIRNS, QUEENSLAND, AUSTRALIA

This Panther Ausf. A is now on display at the Australian Armour and Artillery Museum in Cairns, Queensland. The hull and turret were fabricated by the Hermann Goring Steel Works in Linz, Austria, but the final assembler is unknown due to the loss of its original hull number. The original German hull number was obliterated when it was given a new French AMX hull number, following its post-war refurbishment by the AMX factory. It is believed that this tank served with the French Army 501–503rd RCC, then it went to the Saumur Museum and then went to the Cadman collection before being sold to the Australian Armour and Artillery Museum in 2017. This photograph was taken in 2009 at the War and Peace event, Kent, England, before its restoration. Bruce Crompton's team at axistrackservices.com restored this Panther back to working condition.

This Panzer V Ausf. A Panther tank will be on display at the Australian Armour and Artillery Museum.

PANTHER AUSF. A, CANADIAN WAR MUSEUM, OTTAWA, CANADA

This Panther Ausf. A is on display in the Canadian War Museum, Ottawa, Canada. After its capture, it was shipped to Canadian Forces Base Borden and was on outdoor display until the Department of National Defence's Directorate of History and Heritage, CFB Borden, and the Base Borden Military Museum donated it to the museum in 2005.

The Panther took part in the VE Day (Victory in Europe) celebrations on Sparks Street in Ottawa on 8 May 1945. Therefore, it had to have been transported from Europe before the end of the war, but whether as a war trophy or for testing and experimentation by the military remains unknown. Its restoration was completed in January 2008 and went on public display.

This Panzer V Ausf. A Panther tank is on display in the Canadian War Museum.

PANZER V AUSF. G, PANTHER TRAINING TANK AT FORT BENNING, GEORGIA, USA

See Chapter 3.

PANZER V AUSF. G, PANTHER TANK AT FORT BENNING, GEORGIA, USA

See Chapter 4.

PANTHER AUSF. G, THE TANK MUSEUM, BOVINGTON, DORSET, ENGLAND

This Panzer Ausf. G Panther is on display at the Tank Museum, Bovington, Dorset. It does not have the later gun mantlet with the 'chin guard'. The construction process was finished at the end of the war, in Germany, under the direction of the British Army REME. They completed five Panthers and five Jagdpanthers for testing. These vehicles were already off the production line and in the finishing hall at the MNH factory when activities ceased due to power loss and bombing. Those that did not go to museums and private collections were used as hard targets on the Lulworth live firing range.

This Panzer V Ausf. G Panther tank is on display at the Tank Museum in Bovington.

PANTHER AUSF. G (NO. 801), *WEHRTECHNISCHE DIENSTSTELLE*, TRIER, GERMANY

This Panther Ausf. G (No. 801) is on display at the *Wehrtechnische Dienststelle* in Trier, Germany. It is fitted with a reproduction of the FG 1250 *Nachtsichtgerät* infrared system. The construction process was finished at the end of the war, in Germany, under the direction of the British Army REME. They completed five Panthers and five Jagpanthers for testing. These vehicles were already off the production line and in the finishing hall at the MNH factory when activities ceased due to power loss and bombing. Those that did not go to museums and private collections were used as hard targets on the Lulworth live firing range. This one was previously used as a training exhibit at the British Army Defence Academy in Shrivenham before being transferred to the *Wehrtechnische Dienststelle*. It is in a running condition.

PANTHER AUSF. G, THE FLICK PRIVATE COLLECTION, NORTHERN GERMANY

This Panther Ausf. G is in the Flick Private Collection in Heikendorf, Northern Germany. In July 2015, the German Government seized it from the seventy-eight-year-old owner's basement as it is alleged he did not have the correct German licenses to keep such a vehicle.

The construction process was finished at the end of the war, in Germany, under the direction of the British Army REME. They completed five Panthers and five Jagpanthers for testing. These vehicles were already off the production line and in the finishing hall at the MNH factory when activities ceased due to power loss and bombing. Those that did not go to museums and private collections were used as hard targets on the Lulworth live firing range.

It was purchased by Hardwicks Scrap Metal following a sale by the British War Department in the 1950s. It was kept at their scrap metal yard in Cox Lane in Chessington, Surrey. In 1977, it was sold to *Herr* Flick and transported to Germany, where it was restored to a working condition.

This Panzer V Ausf. G Panther tank (No.801), is on display at the *Wehrtechnische Dienststelle*.

This Panzer V Ausf. G Panther tank is in the Flick Private Collection, in Heikendorf, Northern Germany.

PANTHER AUSF. G (NO. 222), OORLOGSMUSEUM, OVERLOON, THE NETHERLANDS

This Panther Ausf. G (No. 222) is on display in the Oorlogsmuseum, Overloon, the Netherlands. Its hull number, 128427, shows that it was assembled July 1944 in the MNH factory. It belonged to the Pz. Brig. 107.

Panther Ausf. G (No. 222) was later fully restored externally and painted in *dunkelgelb*. It was moved to a new location within the Oorlogsmuseum. This tank's hull number is *Fahrgestell Nummer* 128427, which identifies this as the 327th produced Panther *Ausführung* G tank assembled by the MNH factory in Hannover in early August 1944. It had served on the Eastern Front. It was later sent west after the Allies landed in Normandy. It saw action in the Battle of Eindhoven.

It was hit by a British PIAT during the battles around Overloon, which lasted from September till October 1944. Two pairs of road-wheels were knocked off, leaving the vehicle immobile. The crew abandoned the tank as they could not repair it.

Initial attempts by the museum to arrange for the tank to be restored to a running condition ceased. The engine was sold to the Weald Foundation in England to use in their Jagdpanther.

The Panzer V Ausf. G Panther tank (No. 222) is on display in the *Oorlogsmuseum*. Here you can see it painted in an 'Ambush' camouflage pattern without its tracks fitted before its recent restoration. (*Massimo Foti*)

The Panzer V Ausf. G Panther tank (No. 222) is on display in the *Oorlogsmuseum*. Panther Ausf. G (No. 222) was later fully restored externally and painted in *dunkelgelb*.

PANTHER AUSF. G, HOUFFALIZE, BELGIUM

This Panzer V Ausf. G Panther Tank took part in the Battle of the Bulge. It is on display in the village of Houffalize, Belgium. You will find it at the junction of the N30 Rue de Bastogne with the Rue Saint-Roch. The Houffalize Panther Ausf. G tank originally had the turret number 111 and was part of the Pz.Regt I./24; it was with Pz.Regt I./16 when it was knocked out.

According to statements by veterans and residents, the tank fell over due to detonation pressure by dropped bombs into the Ourthe river and landed on the turret. The crew died because of the impact or drowned.

This Panther was recovered out of the Ourthe by French engineers on 20 September 1947. The remains of the crew killed in the attack were discovered when the Panther was pulled from the river. It was left on the banks of the river for many years and used as a playground by the local children. Many original parts were taken off the tank as souvenirs. It displayed the late war camouflage scheme of green, dark red, and *dunkelgelb*.

When it was first placed on display in the town at the top of the high street, a large German black and white cross was painted on the side of the turret, and the numbers 111 were painted in small numbers along the bottom edge of the turret towards the rear. It was later repainted with a similar three-tone camouflage scheme, but the turret was given the number 401 and painted with the '*Windhund*' insignia of the 116 Panzer Division. In 2017, it was removed to the Bastogne Barracks for restoration.

This photograph of the Panzer V Ausf. G Panther Tank on display in the village of Houffalize was taken before it was moved to Bastogne for restoration.

PANTHER AUSF. G, GRANDMENIL, BELGIUM

This Panther Ausf. G is used as a memorial in Grandmenil, Belgium. It is near the roundabout on the N807 at the junction with the Rue Alphonse Poncelet. This Panther took part in the Battle of the Bulge, Ardennes offensive. It is believed that it belonged to the 2nd SS Panzer Division '*Das Reich*' and was abandoned. It was recovered in a field off the Manhay–Érezée road where five Panther tanks had been damaged by anti-tank mines. It still has its engine and gearbox.

This Panzer V Ausf. G Panther tank is on display in Grandmenil.

PANTHER AUSF. G, CELLES, BELGIUM

This damaged Panther Ausf. G is used as a monument in Celles, Belgium. The Celles Panther was part of the German Army *Kampfgruppe* (combat group) von Cochenhausen, 2nd Panzer Division. On 21 December, Panzer Lehr battle group was pulled out of the fight for Bastogne and regrouped with 2nd Panzer Division and the 116th Panzer Division *Windhund* for an assault on the town of Dinant to secure the crossing over the river Meuse. It fought its way through the town of St Hubert, and the road to Dinant seemed open. Rochefort was taken on 23 December 1944.

On 24 December 1944, the advance column of Panther tanks approached the junction of the N510 road with the N48. The local story is that the Germans asked at the café 'Pavillon des Ardennes' if the road to Dinant was open and whether vehicles had been using it recently. Marthe Monrique, the café owner, lied and said that it was mined and dangerous, so the Panzer V commander decided to go through the fields. This Panzer V Ausf. G was the lead tank. It drove over a mine and was put out of action in the field below the Chateau Acteau. The Germans stopped their advance for a while. After the war, Marthe Monrique became known as the woman who stopped the tanks.

Left: This damaged Panzer V Ausf. G Panther tank is used as a monument in Celles. (*Pierre-Olivier Buan*)

Below left: This photograph shows the damaged caused by an American armour piercing round bouncing off the turret and lower gun mantel armour and smashing its way into the roof above the machine gunner's position on the Celles Panther. (*John Osselaer*)

Above right: The white circle marks out where the American armour-piercing shell hit just below the gun mantlet and then smashed into the hull roof above the bow machine gunner's position. You can also see the scooping effect of other rounds that failed to penetrate the Panther's upper front glacis plate. (*John Osselaer*)

When Panzer Lehr resumed its advance to Dinant, it ran into the Combat Command 'A' of the US 2nd Armored Division near Buissonville. On Christmas Day, the protective winter thick cloud cover disappeared, and the full force of the Allies' air power was deployed, bringing the Panzer divisions to a virtual standstill. The majority of 2nd Panzer's tanks, under Major Ernst von Cochenhausen, had become surrounded near the town of Celles.

On 26 December 1944, the rest of Panzer Lehr made two attempts to relieve them, but they were turned back by Allied fighter bombers. Major Cochenhausen and 600 or so of his men managed to escape on foot, having been forced to abandon all of the division's tanks and equipment to the advancing Allies.

The disabled Panther at Celles was left there for some time after the war. It had flipped over and was resting on its turret by the side of the road to Neufchateau. It was during this period that the hatches, tracks, and road-wheels were removed as they were easy to get to.

The Americans tested anti-tank weapons on it. The café owner Marthe Monrique rescued the tank from the field in 1948 and put it in pride of place next to the café, now renamed as '*Le Tank*' at the crossroads as a monument.

PANTHER AUSF. G (NO. 332), MUSÉE DES BLINDÉS (MUSEUM OF ARMOUR), SAUMUR, FRANCE

This Panther Ausf. G (No. 332) is on display at the *Musée des Blindés*. Its hull number is *Fahrgestell Nummer* 120790, built by the MAN factory at the end of July 1944. The French *2e Division Blindée* (2nd Armoured Division) captured several intact Panthers from I./Pz.Rgt.29 of Panzer Brigade 112 during the fighting at Dompaire on 13 September 1944. Two were sent back to Paris as presents to General de Gaulle to commemorate the victory. Panther 332 sat outside Hôtel National des Invalides in Paris for some years (along with a Panther Ausf. A abandoned in the Jardin du Sénat, Paris, in August 1944) and then sent to Saumur in 1976. The other Panther from the Invalides, an Ausf. A, is now on display at Mourmelon-le-Grand.

This Panzer V Ausf. G Panther tank (No. 332), is on display at the *Musée des Blindés*. (*Massimo Foti*)

PANTHER AUSF. G, KUBINKA TANK MUSEUM, RUSSIA

This Panther Ausf. G tank is on display at the Kubinka Tank Museum, Russia, but may be moved to the nearby Patriot Park tank museum. During restoration work on a fuel tank, the serial or production number 887/44 was found. As you can see, original *Zimmerit* (anti-magnetic mine paste) is still on the tank. *Zimmerit* ceased to be applied to Panther tanks in September 1944. Therefore, it is possible to work out that this tank's hull number was 120887 and built by MAN in August 1944.

This Panzer V Ausf. G Panther tank was photographed on display at the Kubinka Tank Museum.

PANTHER AUSF. G, THE HOEBIG PRIVATE COLLECTION, GERMANY

A Panther Ausf. G tank is believed to be part of the Hoebig Private Collection. This information has not been verified. No photographs have been published.

SURVIVING GERMAN *BERGEPANTHERS* (ARMOURED RECOVERY VEHICLES) (SD.KFZ 179)

The *Bergepanther* was an armoured recovery vehicle that was used by the German Army during the Second World War. It was based upon the hull of the Panzer V Panther. The turret was not fitted. For defence, it could be armed with a 20-mm KwK 38 tank gun and a 7.92-mm MG 34 or MG 42 machine gun. It was equipped with a 40,000-kg winch and cable system.

An early *Bergepanther* Ausf. D is awaiting restoration in Cadman Collection in Southern England. A *Bergepanther* Ausf. A hull is now at the Krings Collection in Germany, pending restoration into a working vehicle. Internal parts have been obtained from the Houffalize Battle of the Bulge War Memorial tank. A *Bergepanther* Ausf. G is stored in the André Becker Collection in Belgium. It is also awaiting restoration.

A restored *Bergepanther* Ausf. A can be seen at the *Wehrtechnische Dienststelle* Museum in Trier, Germany. It was the last Panther produced at the Daimler-Benz production plant in Berlin. There is a shot through the rear plate. It was taken to France after the war and used for testing land mines at the ETBS in Bourges, France. When it was no longer required for trials, it first went to the *Musée des Blindés* in Saumur with two others and then moved to the *Wehrtechnische Dienststelle*, where it was restored. The large spade at the rear was copied and rebuilt at Rheinmetall, Germany.

A restored *Bergepanther* Ausf. G is on display at the *Musée des Blindés*, being transferred there in 1972 from Camp Satory. The winch is operational. The 20-mm machine gun and mount were added later. It was found in a barn in Normandy by someone from the museum.

This restored *Bergepanther* Ausf. A can be seen at the *Wehrtechnische Dienststelle*.

This *Bergepanther* Ausf. G is on display at the *Musée des Blindés*.

BIBLIOGRAPHY

Jentz T. L. and Doyle H. L., *Panzer Tracts No. 23* (Boyds, Maryland, USA: Panzer Tracts, 2001)

Jentz T. L. and Doyle H. L., *Panzer Tracts No. 5-1* (Boyds, Maryland, USA: Panzer Tracts, 2003)

Jentz T. L. and Doyle H. L., *Panzer Tracts No. 5-2* (Boyds, Maryland, USA: Panzer Tracts, 2003)

Jentz T. L. and Doyle H. L., *Panzer Tracts No. 5-3* (Boyds, Maryland, USA: Panzer Tracts, 2004)

Jentz T. L. and Doyle H. L., *Panzer Tracts No. 5-4* (Boyds, Maryland, USA: Panzer Tracts, 2006)

Spielberger W. J., *Panther and its Variants* (Atglen, Pennsylvania, USA: Schiffer Publishing Ltd, 1993)

Schwarzmann, P., *Panzerketten: Die Gleisketten der deutschen Kettenfahrzeuge des Zweiten Weltkriegs* (Brandenburgisches/Siegler, 2013)

Winner, J., *Fgst. Nr. Panther Tanks and Panther 1944.de, production volume and Zuweisungsliste*

The Research Squad, *The Panther Project: Volume One: Drivetrain and Hull* (AFV Modeller, 2018)

The Research Squad, *The Panther Project: Volume Two: Engine and Turret* (AFV Modeller, 2018)